NO MAN'S Concubine

*Tell The Concubine She Was
Meant To Be A Queen*

BEVERLY D. ALLEN

Gotham Books

30 N Gould St.
Ste. 20820, Sheridan, WY 82801
https://gothambooksinc.com/

Phone: 1 (307) 464-7800

© 2025 *Beverly D. Allen*. All rights reserved.

No part of this book may be reproduced, stored in a retrieval system, or transmitted by any means without the written permission of the author.

Published by Gotham Books (April 23, 2025)

ISBN: 979-8-3492-4074-4 (H)
ISBN: 979-8-3492-4072-0 (P)
ISBN: 979-8-3492-4073-7 (E)

Because of the dynamic nature of the Internet, any web addresses or links contained in this book may have changed since publication and may no longer be valid.

The views expressed in this work are solely those of the author and do not necessarily reflect the views of the publisher, and the publisher hereby disclaims any responsibility for them.

This book is dedicated to my jewel from the Lord, my mother, Mrs. Juliette Caldwell, known as Mother Caldwell in our church. You have always been there for me, through every failed turn and every uphill success with loving kind motivation and a powerful prayer life. Thank you for being an example of the unassuming power of a QUEEN and a godly woman-never resorting to be a CONCUBINE, despite the trials and the wiles of the devil.

Thank you for holding on to "your faith in God"-believing that your change would come and staying there when others would have given up on life. You are truly my earthly hero, whom I love and take this opportunity to tell the world in print that you honored "motherhood" and made countless sacrifices for which I could never totally reciprocate in this life-nor would you expect me to. But you know that I am here for you always. I am the woman you say you are proud of, because of God's grace and the example He gave me in you.

Thank you, Mommy. I love you so much!

TABLE OF CONTENTS

Acknowledgements vi
Who Would Write Such A Book? vii
From The Heart of The Author xii
Introduction xv
CHAPTER ONE: "Being A Queen Versus Being A Concubine" . 1
   Born To Be A Queen 2
   Being A Queen Vs. Being A Concubine 4
   The Concubine 7
   Why Be A Concubine When You Can Be A Queen? 10
   The Fate of The Concubines 12
   Don't Let This Happen To You! 15
   A Victim of War - Satan's Tactic 21
   Poverty Is No Excuse 22
   Did You Volunteer? 24
   He's Not Your King, If You're Not His Queen 26
CHAPTER TWO: "Let's Talk About Sex" 29
   Let's Talk About Sex 30
   The Theology of Sex 32
   Sex Is Holy, Sex Is Sacred 35
   Why Marriage? 37
   Marriage - A Sacred Covenant 42
CHAPTER THREE: "The Courtship" 47
   The Courtship 48
   How About A Date 51
   How About The Courtship? 58
   Don't Give Away Your Flavor 60
   Bad Company In The Church 62

Don't Go There!.. 64
Let Sleeping Dogs Lie 65
Which Magazine Did You Read? 68

CHAPTER FOUR: Your Choice in Men.................................... 73
Your Choice In Men 74
Rahab Got A Good Man 76
Jacob Is No Candidate -Yet 79
You Can't Change Jacob 81
Judging His Spirit 82
Sister To Sister... 83
The Flavor of Favor 89
Don't Play with A Player... 95
Wait, Wait, Wait, Again I Say Wait! 100
Waiting... 104

CHAPTER FIVE: Some Things You Need To Know.............. 106
Some Things You Need To Know 107
What You Don't Know Can Hurt You!................................. 109
It's Not Too Late To Say No! 113
No More Toys or Gadgets.. 116
A Lesson From Two Women 119

CHAPTER SIX: The Bite of The Vampire 123
The Bite of The Vampire 124
Bitten By Love? 131

CHAPTER SEVEN: Your Decisions 134
Your Decisions... 135
It's Time To Change Masters 138
Where Is Your Faith?... 140
It's Your Decision: Queen or Concubine............................... 142
My Decision 144

v

Acknowledgements

- First and foremost, to my Lord and Savior Jesus Christ for His divine Spirit's leading to proclaim in writ to His daughters the royal place they have in His Kingdom. I bless His holy name for my salvation and His wondrous "Love" and keeping power over and in my life. Living for Him is a most blessed life and a privilege.

- To Bishop Joseph Allen, my husband, my companion, and friend

- To Evangelist Laura (Viola) Brunson, who led me to Christ, taught me how to fast and pray

- To Jim & Mae Murray

- To my Sister, Sandra Gillead and my niece, Sonya L. Caldwell

May God bless you all for your labor of love and prayerful station over this project to see it come into fruition.

Who Would Write Such A Book?

Who would write such a book? A woman who had been looking for love and a father at the same time, often getting the two confused; sometimes finding one or the other at different times, which was always wrong. It was not until Christ began to draw me to Him through the recognition of my unsuccessful search. I would ask how the Ophelia DeVore School of Charm graduate, Most Outstanding Student (June 1967), could wind up in a search leading nowhere when I had been prepared for much more.

Sin can be glamorous and still be sin in white-collar circles as well as blue collar or no collar zones. Thank God for my older brothers, Rodney and Jimmy, who had been raised to protect their sisters at all costs. Many times, they did just that. But they couldn't protect my heart.

I seemed to be all right until high school graduation, a time when my father was not around. He had left and I felt so unprotected and worst, unwanted because he was not there for "me." He had been around for all the previous graduation celebrations of my older siblings, but now his baby girl was coming out and he was not there! This began the search for my identity and a father's love. I was looking for someone to rescue me. I thought it was from my living circumstances, but it was actually from my hidden loss of self-esteem. I thought my rescue would have to come from an older more mature man.

Wrong! I had some handsome college-bound young men who were seriously interested in me but I fanned them away. There were some other good prospects that I sent away because they weren't enough. They could not offer me what I had missed from my father security and affirmation.

Well, the man I thought fit the bill was not necessarily he. He was much older than I was, handsome and fatherly combined with being someone to love and receive love from in return. From this relationship came a beautiful son who I love. Although I was independent and strong-willed, I was not experienced enough to raise him appropriately. But fortunately for us both, I had a loving wonderful mother. She encouraged me and helped me even though I had not taken her advice and direction which would have delayed motherhood for me. Above all, there was a gracious God who directed me, countering my falls.

The man I fell in love with lived a double life. He was a successful smart liquor salesman by day and a more successful drug dealer by night with celebrity clients and the like. He was well connected and could purchase kilos of cocaine and convert them into thousands of dollars in street sales. As I think of the Grace of God and how He delivered my heart and my life from this connection, it amazes me. My male friend never asked me to cooperate or participate in sales, because I was not only scared, but I was against it. I loved him but not what he did.

That relationship crumbled without my help. When he approached me to be a storehouse keeper for his supplies, I didn't hesitate to tell him no, though it would have meant sharing the profits: cars, jewels, and all the trinkets, which would have been my rewards. He had a friend who was a well-known racketeer but also the father of one my girlfriends. We talked and in a fatherly way, he told me, "Remember, when they come through the door, love is not going to matter. They will take you and your child!"

That was good fatherly advice. Thank God, He used my girlfriend's father to remind me of some consequences I was not willing to pay! My reply of "no" to him was the dissolution of our relationship. I truly bless God that He gave me the strength and good sense to say no to someone I loved. I also recognized that if he had loved me, he would not have asked me to put his son or I in such a position. It didn't hurt him he went on to his other sources. I was very independent at that time. So, with some government assistance for a little while and an honest work ethic, we got on our feet and after a few more knocks, ups and downs, the Lord dealt with me. As the songwriter wrote, *I went to a meeting one night and my heart wasn't right, but something got a hold of me.*

My mother had invited me to a revival meeting at her church. That experience changed the course of my life. My parents had raised us all in the church St. Peter's Baptist Church. But when my father left my mother, all of that went out the window. Even though I went to Sunday school, I didn't know that one's sins (all of them) could be forgiven. I had counted all of mine and said it was too late for me. As a grown young woman, I was afraid to sleep in the dark, afraid to die!

But now I realize that the Lord used that fear to open my ears to hear him calling me. I had been attending church but this one night, a Pentecostal evangelist ran a revival. I had witnessed what was happening to the young people in the church, who were being filled with the Spirit of God. I had been praying that if it was real, I wanted it too. If it wasn't real I was going to expose it as false testimony. But an older Evangelist, Laura (Viola) Brunson, who accompanied the preacher, read my heart and had him pray for me. I was not filled that night, but I began a new relationship with the Lord and had such a hunger and thirst for Him within me! Was it really possible that all my sins could be wiped out? "Yes"! How happy I was to know this wonderful answer.

Evangelist Brunson lived in the area and God used her to teach me more about the Lord. She gave me my first pair of walking shoes in Christ. I learned to seek God, fast and pray, in her little storefront church. While I was praying in her church, God filled me with His Spirit. From that day, the Lord was the Love of my life. My friends and family thought I had lost my mind. I had to let go of the old life and I received a new mind.

Learning how to walk with the Lord, I didn't dot every "i" or cross every "t", but I knew I could repent, confess, and forsake my sins and be forgiven and cleansed. I was waiting to be blessed with a husband who would be good for my son and me. The devil knows it and was still trying to keep me from my purpose and destiny. But God had plans for us and they were for good and not for evil.

A preacher I knew had introduced me to someone who was supposed to be a suitable contender. *"WRONG"!* What baggage and issues he was dealing with in himself. Still, we became engaged. The wedding gown had been purchased and the invitations had gone out and in prayer, God said "No."

I was really seeking Him because I was saved, and I really wanted to do it right. But I never anticipated God saying, he's not the one. He must have said it sooner and I wasn't really listening and not reading the signs. But thank God, I heard Him when I did. I went to one of the deacons of the church and spoke to him and his wife. They encouraged me not to be afraid to call it off. What a relief I felt. I did call it off and had to tell everyone, there would be no wedding. It should have been embarrassing, but it wasn't. I felt free.

So, I was ready to give up looking any longer because I was raising a son. I had my own place, my own car, and a job to support us. Above all, I had faith in the Lord who promised He would never leave me nor forsake *me (Hebrews 5:11)*. I didn't need a knight in shining armor. I needed a godly man who would be a good husband and an honorable father my son could be around without fear. I also made up my mind and said, "Forget about it, Lord. It will be you, me, and the son you have blessed me to have."

But a year later, I went to our organization's national meeting in Atlanta, GA. At that conference, I met the man who the Lord would send to be my partner and friend. He was my Salmon, for he was a prince **in** the kingdom of God, my Joseph, and as they say, "the rest is history." Only the Lord could do this. Had I not surrendered to his call, I would have settled to continue as a "Concubine" when the Lord had called me to be a "Queen." That is what He desires for each of His daughters and nothing less with or without a mate.

So don't settle, don't lower your expectations or your standards. Let the words ahead encourage you to trust in the Lord and know that no matter where you are or where you have been, Christ loves you and wants more for you than you could ever want for yourself.

If you have all your degrees, and your bank account is full, His expectations for you exceed that, for they are greater spiritually and naturally!

From The Heart of The Author

I want to share some personal thoughts about why I believe the Holy Spirit inspired me to do this labor of love. The attempt as writer is not to judge, but to enlighten and encourage the daughters of God and show them who they are in Christ. It is time to understand your position as a born-again child of God through Christ, King of Kings, as a "QUEEN" walking in your new birthright.

I hope that my sisters in Christ, who love the Lord, share this book. They may yet have struggles with their flesh to the point of surrendering to the will or are close to surrendering to the desires of the flesh. This is the clarion call to your spirit directing you not to surrender and settle for becoming a "CONCUBINE" when it is really your time to be a "QUEEN." Your Father wants you to know you are His Queen and He wants more for you than you even want for yourself!

The inspiration of what appears in the following pages is what I wish I had had before I was Born Again (Saved). The truth of scriptures and the direction of the Word of God are a blessing to the doers of the word, and the door to many more blessings. One of the problems for many young girls is what she does when her father leaves home (or maybe never was in the home) at a critical time before he even validated her worth. Perhaps, he had not admonished her to keep herself for her husband or was not there to protect her from many of the abuses that come when no strong man is around to dissuade any possible assaulters. What she may actually do is go on a search for such a man, having one disappointment after another. Maybe, she gave up hope forever of finding one who can love her as she desires to be loved.

No matter how old she is, no matter how successful or unsuccessful she may be, there is great and glorious hope through **CHRIST!** Sure, you have heard this before, by the scriptures, we overcome by the Blood of the lamb and the word of our testimony. Accept this as a personal testimony to the glory of God. Nothing is too hard for God and all things are possible if you believe and respond to the direction of His word for your life.

I was a single woman, who as a young girl experienced the separation of my parents. Actually, my father took off, leaving me and I say me because he left when I was the last child and the youngest at home (which didn't add to my self-esteem) at that time. He left before he had actually packed his clothes. He was living a double life between two households, married to two women (as we learned at the time of his expiration).

So, with the help of a loving mother and faithful wife, who sacrificed everything for her children and even cared for his sickly parents, despite her battle with cancer when I was about eleven years old, I stumbled through, trying to find my true identity. Sadly, this road took me to heartbreak and disappointment. But it also led me to one who said, "I'll never leave you nor forsake you, and I am a good Father who knows how to give good gifts to his children.

I have made my share of mistakes, had enough failures, and experienced enough of the bright side of life at various times to be able to encourage someone else that, despite the areas of life that make us ashamed of the past, you were predestined to be a QUEEN through Christ. Those of us who are born into the royal family, the chosen generation and royal priesthood are the children of the King, not figuratively but literally.

This is a position that mandates certain behavior and requires you to receive new knowledge, for often God's people are destroyed for a lack of knowledge. Now, as I look back in hindsight, I want to tell someone in my position about life, men, God and themselves. I would like to speak words of life to your spirit. I want to refute the voice of the enemy when he tells you, because of your failure in the area of holding on to your virginity, and a past strewn with more experiences than you would like to admit to, that there is yet restoration and joy reserved for you.

Yes, this includes those who are serving in the church as well as those outside of Christ. You can get back what the Devil stole. You don't have to want less because of your sins committed while serving the Lord. There is enough "GRACE" and mercy for cleansing from the guilt and shame of what you have done, for He is faithful and just to forgive us of our sins and cleanse us from all <u>unrighteousness</u>! It is time to take back the rule from the enemy and place it in the hands of the Lord. By His word and through His Spirit in you, claim the joy unspeakable full of glory He has for you!

I also want to say to the widows especially, that God has not forgotten you. He has made provision and continues to make ways for you. If you focus on Him and His righteousness, He will send you joy through a Boaz or a Ruth. He will make you smile again. Don't leave the place of blessing to get temporary "deliverance."

Go through whatever tests or vicissitudes of life you face, for God has a purpose and a plan for you in your present state. Do not miss and do not run from it, for the end will be greater than the beginning.

Be encouraged and not intimidated by where you are now. Be a "QUEEN" at every valley, bump, curb, and don't stop as you walk with Christ. You are accepted in the beloved and chosen before the foundation of the world!

Introduction

The Church of the Lord Jesus Christ is universally full with women who love their Lord and Savior, desire to work toward the up building of His Kingdom, are faithful to their local churches, pay tithes, go to Bible class, and study the Word of God. Yet, they limit themselves and the power they have been endowed with to wait on the Lord to bless them with the mate He has created for them or to serve as single maids in service.

The scriptures tell us that, "a single woman careth for the things of the Lord," because she doesn't have the distractions that a married woman would have. That is, if she is called to singleness, and I do believe that some women and men may be called to singleness without being uncomfortable in their flesh.

Disobedience is not always done deliberately or defiantly, but for various reasons, which still add up to disobedience. I believe revelation is powerful and that it will deliver a soul from disobedience in any area that hinders the plans or delays the plans.

God has a plan for His daughters. The daughters of God, the King of Glory, are royalty and ultimately "QUEENS" by a new birth and their covenant relationship to **CHRIST**. While they have this wonderful position available to them, they live beneath their privilege and have settled for the life of a "concubine." Any woman who is having conjugal relations with a man without a legal, legitimate marital covenant agreement is operating in the spirit of the concubine. God does not ordain the secondary position. Some of God's chosen leaders participated in this type of relationship, but without God's sanctions or approval.

The bride of Christ is the Church, and the Bible tells us whatever we do in word or deed, we are to do it all in the name of "JESUS." We operate in the matchless name of the one who died for us. We pray, preach, worship, teach, rebuke, forgive, and all things pertaining to our approach to God in the name of Jesus. That's our privilege as his espoused bride. The marriage relationship is a type of Christ's relationship with the Church.

To have a partner who will not offer to marry you, which would entitle you to his name and his commitment to share everything that belongs to him is not true love. Anything less is leaving the back door open to escape when he is tired of playing house or wants an updated playmate. He doesn't truly want to be partnered with you for a lifetime. He only wants a concubine, someone like a wife a secondary wife, someone who will have children without a commitment, who will cook for him without a commitment, clean for him without a commitment, give their youth-strength-emotions etc. without a commitment. He wants you to have less than what Christ has promised you, His very best.

You and you alone will decide whether you will be his concubine or whether you qualify to be his QUEEN. Read further and you will have help in realizing that you are who God says you are a new creation from a chosen generation of a royal priesthood. Your position as a concubine is not determined by your education, (for many concubines are well educated today), nor by your beauty, your financial status, or any other superficial thing, but only by your faith in God and His word for your life.

This book is not to condemn but to encourage, enlighten and awaken the daughters of the kingdom to arise to their established position that Christ shed His blood for you to inherit.

CHAPTER ONE

"Being A Queen Versus Being A Concubine"

Born To Be A Queen

To this world I was born royalty

Being groomed and molded to fulfill the steps of being a Queen

No ideals or thoughts of being common were allowed to flow

Through the canals of my mental stream

Along the way somehow my royal steps turned dim

My royal glow lost its shine

For I have allowed myself to believe a lie

That I was not in fact born to be a Queen

But to be a slave and live out my life playing second, third or even fourth as a concubine

The crown that once adorned my head

Lay tarnished for all to see

Not on the top of my head but at my feet...

Mirrors remain broken...

For I cannot stand to see myself

What a lie and what a fallacy I believed

When I stopped reaching for the throne

And found myself laying and waking up with dirt, rocks and stones

The life and times of a queen turned concubine

Was not the one chosen to be mine?

Thus, I will make the effort to turn my life around

For God says I can heal

And once again regain my crown

By Sonya L. Caldwell

Being A Queen Vs. Being A Concubine

This is not an attempt to give a biblical history of concubinage. It is not to note any particular period when this was practiced.

The goal is to show God's ultimate plan for His daughters and to reveal His intentions. In addition, I want to expose the enemy's present day bondage plan to prevent the spiritual daughters of Abraham from taking their place, having been birthed into their royal family.

You must know what the historical role, life and state of the concubine was, in order to see that the Word of God and the love of God must deliver the present-day spirit of the concubine through sanctification. This spirit has been maintained or nursed by ignorance of her true worth and position by birth into the kingdom of God the royal family of a chosen generation. This birth was not by accident, but predestined, planned before the foundation of the world.

Too many daughters are settling for less than what they have been promised. It's time for them to take their blood bought, blood washed, redeemed place despite their past. The Word of God tells us, "If any man (person) be in Christ he (they) is a new creation old things are passed away and behold all things are become new" *(2 Corinthians 5:17)*. We are also to walk in the newness of life, not the old ways of the world because of the guilt and shame of our past or the lack of faith. We deserve better.

It is this writer's hope that every daughter will be encouraged to receive all that the Lord has already supplied and walk in her new status as a *Queen* never again to settle for being a *"Concubine."* I am writing to tell every girl, young lady or woman living the lifestyle of a concubine while being of the spiritual seed of Abraham that she is a *"QUEEN."* Also to tell all those desiring to become a member of this royal family that they must be prepared to walk in this new status and accept the responsibility of their position.

King David was a boy who tended to his father's sheep. He cared for them, watched over and protected them. At times, he probably slept with them in their sheepfold, when necessary. **His** father was not a king, nor was his brothers' princes in the nation of Israel. Saul, the first King of Israel, was from no royal lineage. There had been no kings in Israel prior to Saul's appointment by God. He was made a king because the people no longer wanted spiritual leaders, like Samuel the prophet. The people cried for a king like other nations. So the office began by appointment. David did not know how to be a king; but God predestined his life that he would be in the presence of one who was a king. He would learn all the manners of kingship.

I share this information with you, sisters, because there is perhaps no one **in** your family who was a queen-or had the mentality of a queen. You may be the first in your family to recognize who you are in the family of God. As a child raised by her mother and never knowing her daddy, it may come as a surprise to learn that he connected you to a host of family members who were from a royal line.

Daughters of the Most High God, your Father is King of Kings and Lord of Lords. Having just come to this understanding, you can no longer live as women who don't know the Lord--or those who have known but refuse to do His Will. You must take your rightful place as a Queen-Whether you are a Queen with no children or a Queen with no King and five or more children. Once you accept who you are and whose you are, there are no alternative choices. As Queen, you must act like one. You are appointed to this position by your new birth in Christ. You must refuse to be a Concubine or secondary wife. This position was never meant for you.

Like David, you may learn that getting to the palace will be preceded by battles with Goliaths and other dangerous foes. But you were predestined to be Queen, born for this and "born again" to rightfully take your place. Don't let your battles keep you from recognizing who God meant for you to be. Tend to your bruises quickly, through the Word of God, allow them to heal as you walk in the steps of your royal position. As you practice your royal responsibilities, you will feel more comfortable and the Queen in you will become more comfortable exercising her rights.

Being a Queen far exceeds being any man's Concubine, because being a Queen is not solely dependent on having a king or a man. *BE A QUEEN!!* Read on for help in recognizing and appreciating where the Lord wants to take you and how He expects you to respond.

Corinthians 10:31 "... whatever ye do, do all to the glory of God." (NASR)

The Concubine

"A woman who co-habits with a man although not legally married to him." (Webster's New World Dictionary/Second College Edition/William Collins & World Publishing Co., Inc., Copyright 1976 and 1974).

Jewish laws define a concubine as a woman dedicating herself to a particular man with whom she co-habits without marriage. A concubine is to be distinguished both, on the one hand from a married woman, by "marriage ceremony" and on the other, from a woman who does not dedicate herself to one particular man exclusively, but who prostitutes herself (i.e. the harlot). *(Encyclopedia of Religion & Ethics-Vol.3&4-edited by James Hastings/Publisher/Scribner/ Copyright, 1928,1950,1961).*

In the ancient Near East, a concubine was a woman bought from a poor family or taken captive in battle to be a man's unmarried companion. Generally, only wealthy men could afford to keep them. Abraham had concubines, as did David. But for sheer numbers, Solomon topped them all. There were seven hundred princesses and three hundred concubines among his wives *(1 Kings 11:3).*

A concubine bore children and was responsible for taking care of some portion of the household. A man was expected to assume the obligations of a husband to his concubine, whom he was not allowed to sell. However, she did not have the same rights as his legal wife. Childless wives, such as Sarah and Rachel, sometimes gave their handmaidens to their husbands as concubines to bear children for them. A concubine's sons could have the same right to inheritance as the sons of wives, which often created tension between the two groups.

The practice of concubinage was widespread in the biblical world. In Mesopotamia, the husband was free to have legal sexual relations with slaves. In Assyria, the husband was able to take several freeborn concubines as well as his "veiled" wife, although the concubine was subject to the wife's authority. Concubines who bore children and who behaved arrogantly could be treated as slaves but not sold *(cf Laws of Hammurabi 146-147; 170 -171)*. Sarah provided a slave concubine for Abraham *(Genesis 16:2-3)* and handmaidens given as marriage gifts to Leah and Rachel, became Jacob's concubines *(Genesis 29:24, Zilpah; Genesis 29:29, Bilhah)*.

Concubines were protected under Mosaic Law *(Exodus 2:7-11; Deut. 21:1014)*, although they were distinguished from *wives (Judges 8:31; 2Samuel 5:13;] 1Kings 11:3; 2Chronicles 11:21)* and were more easily divorced *(Genesis 21:1014)*. The practice of concubinage created tension with the wives in all periods and later prophets encouraged monogamy *(Malachi 2:14)*. The ideal woman of Proverbs 31 belonged to a monogamous society.

The New Testament shows that monogamy was enjoined by Jesus (Matthew 5:32; 19:3-12) and by **N.T.** writers (1 Tim. 3:2,12).

The contemporary world of the Greeks and Romans still practiced concubinage. Concubines among the Greeks were maintained for sexual pleasure. Children born from such unions, although free, were bastards. It was the "wives" who bore legitimate children. In the Roman world, the state of concubinatus, or "lying together," involved informal but more or less permanent unions without a marriage ceremony. Children of such unions took the legal status of their mother and were deprived of the status of citizens. Against such a background, monogamy was the only form of marriage for Christians.

Unmarried men who had a concubine were obliged to marry or be refused baptism; the believing woman would be baptized. In the Middle Ages, concubinage was formally forbidden and considered by the rabbis as immoral. Only one authority, *Jacob *Emden (responsum no. 15)* expressed the opinion that it should be permitted. There is no evidence of actual concubinage in the

Talmud, nor is there any evidence of it being practiced during the Middle Ages.

Among Hebrews and Jews, bond service or slavery was mild and equitable in character. Because of their protection by law, the position of Israelite slaves was easier than that of foreign slaves. Hebrew slave owners or masters were compelled to treat their hired servants not as slaves with rigor and cruelty, but with courteous consideration as brethren. While the Bible records slavery, it nowhere condones it.

All that has been stated before now was to show and demonstrate that the place of a concubine was the position of a *"secondary wife"*, with inferior social and legal standing. A concubine did not have all the rights of a primary wife, but her rights and the rights of her children were well defined and documented in secular sources like the Code of Hammurabi (1750 B.C.)

Why Be A Concubine When You Can Be A Queen?

A Queen: A female member of the royal house, either the wife of a king, or a woman who reigns by her own power.

There were various ways in which girls/women became a concubine or subjected to concubinage:

1- **War** captured by an enemy nation, tribe or people.

2- **Poverty** the father would sell his daughter as a slave to secure provisions to sustain his family, or also to pay a debt.

3- **King** would take extra wives for political reasons, to build military alliances with other nations (daughters of kings and high-ranking officials).

4- **Volunteer** any female needing protection and provision could opt to sell herself as a slave in man's household (usually to a man of great means for himself or his son). She could become a man's mistress or a woman's (queen or of high rank) handmaiden to bear children.

While that was then, many women today have come under the same concubine spirit by similar circumstances. The life of a concubine would appear to be a type of slavery and God made provision for his daughters who would be made slaves because of circumstances beyond their control. It was not the ideal relationship, and God never wanted such a lifestyle for his people, certainly not his daughters. Why? The sexuality of a people was tied to their worship. The God that they served dictated their lifestyles and behaviors. God put on record His character for his people and the world to know, *"be ye Holy for I the Lord your God am Holy."*

The God of Abraham, Isaac, and Jacob created monogamy and were against adultery, fornication and polygamy. It may have happened amongst His people but without His approval or sanction.

The Fate of The Concubines

In the patriarchal period, the taking of a concubine was a symbol of virility and power of tribal chiefs and kings such as Saul who had Rizpah *(2Samuel 3:7, 21:1)*. Others were Gideon had a nameless concubine along with many wives *(Judges 8:31)*, Nahor had Reumah, a slave in his house *(Genesis 22:24)*, and Abraham had Keturah besides Hagar.

Many of these concubines bore children for their masters to ensure family posterity. The importance of women's identity in ancient Israel as daughters, wives and mothers has a great deal to do with survival in the ancient Near East generally during the second and first millennia B.C.E. The survival of the family was important because the people's social organization derived from their perceived needs. The securing of many wives, whom we define in our culture as polygamy, made possible large families that were needed to perform the labor of herding cattle, farming crops, and defending against hostile aggressors. Many women died during childbirth and many infants and children died before reaching adulthood, so the birthing of many offspring was vital to guarantee a family's posterity and, by extension, the people's survival. Women, therefore, perceived their primary task was to bear children along with their participation in other work necessary to ensure the survival of the family. *(Women's Bible Commentary/ Expanded Edition-Newsom Ringe pg.119/Westminster John Knox Press/Copyright 1992,1998)*

In those times, besides times for many of the men's personal gratification, we can see the threat upon the people. Families could become extinct because of death, or war, and other ills. Given the status of women and the opportunities available to them, I understand how their self-esteem could be tied to the number of children birthed-especially the number of boys they would be able to bear for a man.

That doesn't explain why we, as women today, go to lengths to please men without a commitment and a promise to be fathers. Often the woman knows that a man has had children by other women. Yet, she will desire to bear a child while she is with him (as if this will provide some claim to him).

Listen, sisters. This will not bring him honor or your happiness. You will shoulder the full responsibility when he decides to move on. You will become exhausted trying to get him to court for child support. Think about the child who will have the misfortune of having an absentee father, who won't take time to nurture him, care for him and bond with him. This is not fair to the children or to you! But when this is the case, the Lord will be a father to the fatherless and the head of the household. If you have experienced this pain, know that the children you have borne are still gifts from God. Children are an inheritance of the Lord; separate the act from the effects. The act was sinful, yet the results of children are precious in God's sight. The Lord permitted it to be so. Having been born, they each have a destiny and a purpose of God. So, love them as the King's children and take care to raise them with a love and reverence for God. Also take care of yourself, your health and peace of mind to see your children through childhood. They need "you" because God yet has plans for you. Even if their earthly father fails them, their heavenly

Father will not. David encourages us in:

Psalm 27:10 "For my father and my mother have forsaken me, but the Lord will take me up." (NASB)

The Lord will always be a father to the fatherless. Who knows what great and wonderful plans the Lord has for His children. Yes, they are his children, and they are on loan to you, so be very particular how you care for this royal generation. Ask the Lord to grant you wisdom and strength to do it and He will.

If this is not your situation, then don't create a more difficult task for yourself, because life will present enough challenges for you. But if you know a sister who has this plight, don't criticize her. Help her and encourage her in the Lord. There are women who have unintentionally been a concubine for one or more men, having borne children for them. When we see this, we sometimes gasp, Oh how could she let this happen! Well, I would guess the same way some of us could carelessly, without real knowledge of a man, go to bed with him after one date, or after several months, feeling you really know him. After this short period of time, he leaves you crying and asking yourself, what happened? All of these situations happen when we don't follow God's plan for our life outlined in the scriptures.

We must be very careful how we treat one another. The scriptures admonish us to restore those who have fallen with fear knowing that it could be us. We are never that righteous or holy that we could never fall in a different state of affairs, for Paul tells us in the scriptures:

Galatians 6:1 "Brethren, even if anyone is caught in any trespass, you who are spiritual, restore such a one in a spirit of gentleness; each one looking to yourself, so that you too will not be tempted." (NASB)

You have more to do than to be some man's concubine, adding to his ego for power and virility that neither he nor you can afford. In those days, the men who practiced this had the financial means to provide for their children. In today's world, this is not acceptable or legal, if he wants you to have his child because he loves you, then he should marry you and commit to you. Your father, who is King of Kings and Lord of Lords, would have it no other way. By the way he should have the same father and Lord, and you both should be under the counseling of a sincere loving shepherd, a Pastor who is the watcher for your souls. This should be in place before you make a decision.

Don't Let This Happen To You!

Despite the fact that having concubines was an accepted part of Israelite society, it was not what God intended *(Genesis 2:24)*.

God even specified in *Deuteronomy 17:17* that the king of Israel was not to take many wives for himself for it would lead him away from the Lord *(Life Application Bible/NIV)*.

The king must not take many wives for himself, because they will lead him away from the Lord. (Deuteronomy 17:17)

The lifestyle of many of the concubines was not often one of glamour. At times, even the wives had to endure humiliation by their spouses. But at least they had some legal protection and status. A concubine had most of the duties but only some of the privileges of a wife. Despite the concubine's legal attachment to one man, she and her children usually did not have the inheritance rights of the legal wife and legitimate children. Her primary purpose was giving the man sexual pleasure, bearing additional children, and contributing more help to the household or estate.

The concubines were sometimes captures from wars, and at times Israelites in some cases as in *Judges 19:1-29*. Just as we read of many abuse cases of wives and girlfriends, this is not a new trend. These problems for women can be found as far back as Old Testament records.

The story of the Levite's concubine is found in the book of *Judges 19:1-29*. The Levite, like the preacher of today, was not to have a concubine because of his sacred association. But when men's hearts are far from God, there's no telling what they are capable of doing. Sadly, to say, women did not hold the prominent positions they experience today. There were very few Deborah's as a rule, even some Queens. But the majority of women were homemakers, whose main responsibility was the caring of the home and the rearing of children. One of the greatest callings of today is still being a homemaker and raising children, although it may not be esteemed in society, as highly as some other professions. The men were the workers and the means of the family's support.

The story of the concubine in *Judges 19* is sadly one of abuse and defines their value in those days. This nowhere reflects how the Lord felt about women, only how some of the men during this period felt. This was a time when men seemed to be a law unto themselves. This is also reflective of the shameful state to which some of the Israelites, God's people had sunk. Both the Levite and the concubine are unnamed. The scriptures tell us that these things happened when Israel had no king. So, we see leadership was at an all-time low.

The Levite brought home a woman from Bethlehem in Judah to be his concubine. We see what his intentions were for this woman, because a primary wife would have a legal ceremony or ritual performed to declare her as his wife; should he decide to leave her, he would need a letter of divorcement. This would most likely cause him to pay some type of support depending on his reasons. He doesn't show by his actions any commitment toward her, other than having his needs met. The concubine is said to be unfaithful to him and returns to her father's house. We are not told how she was unfaithful, or whether she was caught with another man. Considering the times, we don't know if the Levite made up the story of her unfaithfulness or not. But she went back to her father's house. We don't know how the Levite was treating her. But we see that the Levite went back to get her from her father's house. This secondary wife had inferior rights as his concubine.

Her father was happy to see his son-in-law and was very pleasant, wanting him to stay the night and enjoy himself. It would seem like neither the father nor the Levite were considerate of the woman. She obviously had to return with him and they were going to a town where there were Israelites to spend the night. They were unable to find a place to stay, when an old man invited them to stay at his house in Gibeah, in the territory of Benjamin.

They were on their way to the Tabernacle of the Lord, as a Levite, this man had religious associations. Agreeing to go stay with this kind man, the Levite, his servant and the concubine went along. It was not safe for them to stay in the square all night, the old man pointed out. But as it turned out it was no safer in the old man's house. This city had some wicked men who came and surrounded the house. They began beating at the door and asking to have the men sent out to them.

They wanted these men, just as the wicked men of Sodom and Gomorrah wanted to know the angels visiting their city. For what was about to take place, I will note some background information from the NIV LIFE APPLICATION BIBLE footnote in the book of Judges. The law of hospitality in the Middle East was stronger than any other, though unwritten. At the top of the list was the responsibility for protecting a guest. It is fair to say what happens next is an example of a code turned to fanaticism. Because the old man desired to protect his guests, he offered his daughter who was a virgin and the Levite's concubine to the men.

Could you imagine the headlines today if a man were to make the same offer? Well, the men didn't want to accept the offer. So the Levite pushed his concubine out the door for the men. The men of the town abused her all night long, raping her until morning. If this were not horrible enough, at dawn when they finally let her go, she collapsed at the door and lay there until the light.

When the Levite was hurrying to leave, he saw her face down and told her to get up and let's go! How degrading could this have been, how cold could a heart be? This poor concubine, regardless of her past did not deserve this. He had no empathy, no compassion for what she had been through. He was going to leave her there, not fearing her outcome, but only for his own life.

Well, she died, and the Levite took her back with him home and dismembered her body into 12 parts. He sent one to each of the twelve tribes of Israel, wanting them to help him give retribution to the enemy who had done this to his concubine. He, who caused her death and had little or no respect, now wanted his people to go to war for this crime. My guess is he was trying to save face before his people who knew of her. Perhaps this would be the cover-up. Now, he wants others to risk their lives for her retribution, when he could have saved her life.

This behavior parallels what we read about, hear from the news media, and see in our communities. This behavior crosses cultural and racial lines. There are still many men who disregard the feelings of women and treat them as objects. This concubine was an object to the Levite, for his pleasure and comfort. She may not have had much of a choice, between her father not standing up for her and her master's (the Levite) abusive ways.

When the concubine went back to her father and the Levite came to get her back after four months, her father tried to get him to stay for a while. I wonder if it was because while she was there, he was able to relax and let his daughter take on responsibilities that were normally his.

The Levite sounds like many men who only want a concubine, someone like a wife, without the legal ties and emotional commitment. A woman he can walk away from at any time. A woman who won't demand anything of him and has not decided she should be living the life of a Queen-not knowing that her heavenly Father is not pleased with her settling for such a life. A woman, who has not realized that she has greater purpose and destiny in her, and has little or no knowledge of God's word, will settle.

Therefore, her enemy Satan can speak to her mind and tell her she doesn't deserve more than this. Because of where she's been and whom she has been with, she feels unworthy. These were backslidden Israelites who stopped allowing God to lead them. They couldn't come into the possession of the land God promised because of disobedience; and a lack of trust in Him to keep his promises. They did whatever seemed right in their own eyes. When God was no longer leading them, they became like those around them. There was a great drop in their standards. They constructed laws that would benefit, not judge and correct them. When God is left out of our lives, there is no telling how sinful we are capable of becoming.

God's beloved daughters and my wonderful sisters know that our Lord does not want us in an abusive relationship. He does not want us yoked up with a weak, disobedient, spiritually void man who professes to be **His,** but possesses nothing of his Father.

Jesus said in *St. John 14:15:* "If you love me keep my commandments." When you love someone, you seek to please that person. If a man does not love the Lord, he will not love his Word enough to obey. His Word must set the boundaries in your relationship, and be the final word when either person seeks truth.

God's Word sets the standard of what "love" is and what it is not.

> *"Love is patient, love is kind and is not jealous; love does not brag and is not arrogant, does not act unbecomingly; it does not seek its own, is not provoked, does not take into account a wrong suffered, does not rejoice in unrighteousness, but rejoices with the truth; bears all things, believes all things, hopes all things. Love never fails"*
> *1 Corinthians 13:4-8 (NASB)*

This is the Bible's measuring rod when a person says they love someone. If he says he loves you, judge his spirit by the Word. Love is not just what it says, but what it does. There are times when we want a partner so bad, we settle for any type of companionship. We settle for sex and not love and use one hoping to get the other. Unlike the Levite's concubine, you have a choice now! Choose to do what pleases God. All throughout the scriptures, God blessed his people when they obeyed. When they were disobedient, he allowed them to feel the pain of their choices. Why live like that when you have been chosen to live above that?

Most concubines like Rizpah *(2 Samuel 3:7; 21:1)* and her children, by attachment to a backslidden king like Saul, suffered tremendous heartache. Other concubine's names are mentioned for bearing sons for their master. Abraham's brother Nahor, whose concubine was Reumah, is named along with her six sons borne to Nahor *(Genesis 22; 24; 25:6)*

When the harlot Rahab saved the spies, because she believed the God of Israel was Lord and wanted to be saved along with her family, God gave her a prince. A prince named Salmon was not the greatest honor, but she was also in the lineage of our Lord Jesus Christ; and named in the scriptures. Just as God called Rahab to be a Queen, he is calling his daughters today to their place in Him. Don't let what happened to those concubines happen to you. Remember, you are more than a conqueror in Christ!

A Victim of War - Satan's Tactic

In wars, many children have been left orphaned or fatherless. The Father is to be the protector and guardian of his home and family. Many fathers have left their daughters defenseless and unprotected involuntarily through death. Also some of them were taken captive to drugs, to prison, to other women (or men), or just a selfish lifestyle.

So, the daughter seeking love, provision and protection, did so by any means necessary. Sometimes, this road led to incest or molestation or early sexual promiscuity. Now, having lost respect for their own bodies, they open themselves to anyone who would seemingly give them a false sense of love or security.

Many mothers have added to the problems of their daughter's behavioral confusion as well. This is not to bash fathers, for many fathers have done and are doing an outstanding job raising their daughters. The importance of a father in the life of his daughter cannot be stressed enough!

Satan will try to rage wars in your life and cause you to put yourself in bondage to this lifestyle. Resist it; fight it through prayer and fasting and reading the word of God. Busy yourself with other interests to enhance you and your self-esteem. You have been set free. Don't allow this to put you in bondage, for whom the Son has set free is free indeed!!

Poverty Is No Excuse

Why Did Daddy Do This?

Some fathers sold out their daughters by not teaching them who they were as their daughters. They stayed home but did not involve themselves diligently in the things that make a house a home of love, protection, and provision. No love expressions between mom and dad; instead, arguing and fighting daily. Physical and sexual abuse, as well as verbal abuse that tagged on to the other abuses.

The result: the daughter grows up with a distorted view of a genuine relationship. She will either avoid giving her heart to any man because there is a lack of trust for that gender, or she will give herself physically to a number of men. However, she will withhold her heart as a defense to getting a broken heart. Fathers do set the example of the type of man who will make a good husband for their daughters. Daughters learn best by example. It becomes so easy for Satan to strike a young woman's self-esteem with feelings of inadequacy and a distorted image of herself. Sadly, there are fathers who sell their daughters for a drug habit or for selfish desires. They think that their actions only affect themselves. They don't realize how vulnerable their family is when they leave the place God has designed for them.

But daughters, be of good cheer for as David said:

"Even if my father and mother abandon me the Lord will hold me close". Psalms 27:10 (Life Application Study Bible)

Many children have had the sad experience of being abandoned by a parent or both parents due to broken homes, differences of belief or addiction to drugs or alcohol. Even psychological isolation can leave children crippled by this loss. As adults, the pain may linger. But God can take that place in your life, fill that void and heal that hurt. He can direct us to other adults who take the role of father or mother. God's love is sufficient for all our needs.

When there is no father in the formative years of a girl's life, she is often affected **in** many ways. For some, the absence creates a starvation for male approval, which would have been satisfied by a father's confirmation and approval. So, in the absence of his approval and confirmation, she seeks for it from other boys or men. This sometimes develops into an obsessive need for male affirmation. The normal attraction for a male has become a search for her father's approval or confirmation.

Sex does not, in and of itself, produce love. There is a vast difference between the two. Pure love, as God designed it, can and will produce righteous and holy sex. Most people refer to good sex as that climatic moment when one reaches an orgasmic high. God designed this experience and the gratification experienced is greater when one enjoys it with a covenant partner, someone who purely and solely gives himself to you and you alone. Don't deny yourself this experience and sell yourself short for only fleshly, short-term satisfaction!

Did You Volunteer?

In times past, any female needing protection and provision could opt to sell herself as a slave to a man's household (usually to a man of great means for himself or his son). Today is not very different. Some women feel they should have a man to help provide and protect them, which is not always what they end up doing. It is sad that so many young women with great potential sell themselves short; hoping that shacking up or joining themselves to one man without legal commitment will fulfill their need.

It may be temporarily but watch out! It won't last forever. Then, she goes out on a new search for someone else. In time, the same cycle repeats itself. It may continue until they are hurt deeply enough to say, I can't keep doing this, or something drastic happens. Any woman in this position needs to look to the scriptures for direction and strength to overcome the lies of the enemy. By comparison, the standards of Rome in Jesus' day and today are similarly low. Paul states in *1 Thessalonians 4:1-8* how to possess one vessel (body) in honor:

> *"That every one of you should know how to possess his vessel in sanctification and honor... "1 Thessalonians 4:4 (Dickson NASB)*

Sexual standards were very low in the Roman Empire. In many societies today, they are not any higher. The temptation to engage in sexual intercourse outside the marriage relationship has always been powerful. Giving in to that temptation can have disastrous results. Sexual sins always hurt someone: individuals, families, businesses and churches. Beside the physical consequences, there are also spiritual consequences.

Sexual desires and activities must be placed under Christ's control. God has created sex for procreation and pleasure. He also created it as an expression of love between a husband and wife. The sexual experience must be limited to the marriage relationship to avoid hurting us, our relationship to God, and our relationship with others.

Sexual immorality is a temptation that is always before us in movies and on television. Sadly, sex outside marriage is treated as a normal, even desirable, part of life, while marriage is often shown as confining and joyless. Others may look down upon you negatively for being pure or committed to the scriptures. But God forbids sexual sin because He knows its power to destroy us physically and spiritually. You can't underestimate the power of sexual immorality.

The devastation caused to countless lives, families, churches, communities, and even nations is far too great. Sometimes, the personal cost is irreversible. God wants to protect us from damaging others, and ourselves. So, he offers to fill us our loneliness, our desires with Himself!

He's Not Your King,
If You're Not His Queen

Queen: *A female member of the royal house, either the wife of a king, or a woman who reigns by her own power.*

Tribal chiefs, kings, and other wealthy men generally took concubines. Gideon had a concubine and Saul had at least one concubine named Rizpah. David had many, but Solomon took the practice to its extreme, having 300 concubines, in addition to his 700 royal wives. *Deuteronomy 17:17* forbids this practice to kings, who were symbols of their virility and power. Having intercourse with the concubine of the ruler was an act of rebellion. When Absalom revolted against his father, David, he "went in unto his father's concubines in the sight of all Israel" *(2Samuel 16:22)* on the palace roof. When David returned to the palace, the 10 concubines involved were sent away to live the rest of their lives in isolation *(2Samuel 20:3)*. A concubine, whether purchased or won in battle, was entitled to some legal protection, but was her husband's property. Any woman resorting to this lifestyle need not expect nor demand fidelity or commitment from her King, who would not make her his one and only Queen.

Sisters, you are accepting the status of being his "property" and not in the proud sense of the word. This arrangement is not in line with the scriptures:

> *"... ye wives, be in subjection to your own husbands;" 1 Peter 3:1 (Dickson NASB)*

> *"Wives submit yourselves unto your own husbands as unto the Lord." Ephesians 5:22 (Dickson NASB)*

> *"Husbands, love your wives, even as Christ also*

loved the church and gave himself for it:" Ephesians 5:25 (Dickson NASB)

Just as Christ has one church, each husband was to have one wife, and each wife was to have one husband (unless she married again because her first husband died). Don't settle for being anything less than a Queen, whether married or single! Where there were wives and concubines in one household or separate living arrangements, there were always problems. Sometimes, there was conflict between the women and sometimes between the children. Sometimes both. Men in the Bible had these types of relations, but of their own will and not because they sought God. It was not God's ideal or his perfect will. What might have seemed permissive was not necessarily condoned, for they often reaped the punishment of their own doings!

Men will often gratify their flesh with several women to show their power and so-called virility. Don't be used as an object to confirm their egos. If you do, eventually you will reap the consequences of your own decision.

Journal Page

(What Thoughts Did The Holy Spirit Give You In This Chapter?)

"You were taught, with regard to your former way of life, to put off your old self, which is being corrupted by its deceitful desires. Ephesians 4:22 (NIV)

CHAPTER TWO

"Let's Talk About Sex"

Let's Talk About Sex

In former years, sex was not a discussion that mothers readily had with their daughters comfortably. A girl's menstruation was difficult enough to talk about without bringing sex into play. The most that would be said is, don't do it. Well in this day and time the topic of sex is certainly not taboo anymore. Since God has designed males and females compatible for sex, the church can teach this issue (with parents' consent and presence). This union is one of the most spiritual experiences you can have within the confines of marriage, the covenant relationship. God planned for sex to be enjoyed within the marriage relationship. There will be adverse effects as the result of being engaged in otherwise.

> *Heb.13: 4 "Marriage is to be held in honor among all, and the marriage bed is to be undefiled; for fornicators and adulterers God will judge. (NASB)*

God designed sex between a man and a woman to be the deepest physical pleasure between man and woman. Satan determined to pervert a beautiful act by its misuse outside of the covenant agreement of marriage. But one cannot and should not settle for cheap temporal pleasure that results in condemnation spiritual and possibly physical death.

Satan never shows one the pain and consequences of their decisions to act outside the will of God. Just as he blinded Eve and Adam, he tries to blind the believers to his tactics. But God would not have us to be "ignorant" of his schemes *(2Cor. 2:11)*. Sex is sacred and it is a holy act-one that bonds two people together. In fact, sex is the ultimate bonding process, as the two become one flesh. The bonding process, becoming one with another, is not to be taken lightly. Paul tells us in *1 Cor. 6:15,17 (NASR): "Do you not know that your bodies are members of Christ? Shall 1 then take away the members of Christ and make them members of a prostitute? May it never be!", vs. 17 "But the one who joins himself to the Lord is one spirit with Him."*

So when we engage in immoral sex we bring the spirit of Christ into it. Believers who possess the Holy Spirit abiding within them wherever they are. We must be very careful where we go and where we take the spirit of God already in us.

We will continue to talk about sex in a covenant relationship as God designed it in this chapter. Pray as you read and explore through the scriptures to see sex in the light God intended us to see and experience it.

The Theology of Sex

*"There shall be no whore **(HARLOT)** of the daughters of Israel" Deuteronomy 23:17 (Dickson NASE)*

The Bible reveals an ethical God who gives humans the gift of sexuality whereby they image God when they join together to complement each other as "one flesh." All non-marital sex is outside the boundaries of the will of this ethical God *(Amos 2:6-8)*: where Israel was instructed to reject sex at the pagan shrines.

God's people are expected to exercise self-control, not by asceticism, but by the power of the Holy Spirit, overcoming sexual impulses *(Galatians 5:16-25)*. For the non-celibate, marriage is the only approved outlet for sexual expression (1 Corinthians 7:9; Titus 2:5-6). An individual's sexuality is a vital part of Christian holiness and not a necessary evil to be rejected.

Within marriage, sex is for procreation of children, the enhancement of the one flesh relationship, and the pleasure of the married couple, whose love can be nourished thereby. Outside of the limits established by God, sex becomes an evil and destructive force in the human life, calling for God's redemptive power to deliver humans trapped therein *(Holman Bible Dictionary Pg. 1252/Holman Bible Publishers/Copyright]991)*.

Marital sexual love is both a gift and a responsibility from God to be consecrated by the Word and prayer.

The reference of *Deuteronomy 23:18* to a whore is referring to a "harlot" or prostitute, a woman who exchanges sex for money. In ancient societies, prostitution was accepted, but in Israel it was only tolerated, not sanctioned. No Israelite was to permit his daughter to become a prostitute *(Leviticus 19:20)*, nor were the wages of a prostitute acceptable as a gift to God *(Deuteronomy 23:17,18)*.

Most prostitution was connected to cult fertility gods and worship. The fertility religions of Canaan assumed that the sex acts of their gods and goddesses were responsible for the fertility of fields and herds. When male or female cult prostitutes engaged in sex, the intention was to sexually stimulate their deities. This stimulation would ensure the fertility of the fields and herds, as in *Genesis 38:21 and Deuteronomy 23:17-18*. This is symbolically a representation of idolatry, as in *Numbers 38:21* or materialism, as in *Revelations 17*.

Cult prostitution was an abomination on three counts:

1. It gave immorality religious sanction.

2. It was associated with pagan religions; and

3. It involved an express reliance on magic.

The unmarried daughter of an Israelite, who did turn to prostitution, was to be stoned *(Deuteronomy 22:21)*. The unmarried daughter of a priest, who became a prostitute, was to be burned *(Leviticus 21:19)*.

The New Testament, which rules out all forms of sexual immorality, expresses shock that a Christian would go to a prostitute. The act would pollute the believer, who is Christ's living temple *(1 Corinthians. 6:15,16)*.

Prostitution was not overlooked in God's law. It was strictly forbidden. To forbid this practice may seem obvious today, but it may not have been so obvious to the Israelites. Almost every other religion included prostitution as an integral part of its worship services. However, prostitution makes a mockery of God's original idea for sex, treating sex as an isolated physical act rather than an act of commitment to another. Outside of marriage, sex destroys relationships. Within marriage, if approached with the right attitude, it can be a relationship builder.

God frequently had to warn the people against the practice of extramarital sex.

Today is no different. We still need to hear God's warnings.

Sexual intercourse was designed to be a pleasurable experience before the fall of Adam and Eve. The joy of the two becoming one flesh would produce wonderful fruit after their kind. Everything was to produce after its kind. This wonderful experience between two people who truly loved each other would be the closest example of the joy and happiness experienced when the people of God unite with the God of their Salvation for all eternity. It would be a sacred union and Holy before the Lord.

Sex Is Holy, Sex Is Sacred

The apostle Paul describes the holy aspect of sex as a great mystery since Christ has now been revealed. This mystery is that the intimacy represented in the sexual union of a believing husband and wife is the representation of the intimacy between our SAVIOR and mankind, the Church or Bride of Christ *(Ephesians 5:31-32)*.

Sex is holy because in the oneness of a human groom and bride, the oneness of the groom, Jesus Christ and His bride, the Church, is represented. According to Tim Alan *Gardner (Sacred Sex pg. 19/WaterBrook Press/Copyright 2002),*

> *"Sex provides the hope for good far beyond what most people dream or imagine. It can provide physical pleasure, to be sure, but it is also a way of communicating tenderness, compassion, caring, and love. It is a way of showing our most intimate connection with our mates and a way of showing God's intimate communion with us. But untold millions have also been devastated and even destroyed, either emotionally or physically, through the evils of sex. This evil that is associated with sex comes from the abuse of God's gift, not from the gift itself. God intended sex to be loving and pleasurable, not a source of heartache and destruction. The experience of holy sex is a gift to those who know the One who made it so. It is made no less holy because many have failed to use the gift according to God's created design and intent."*

The Bible tells us in Ephesians 5:31, "For this cause shall a man leave his father and mother and be united to his wife, and the two will become one flesh" (Dickson NASB). Paul is stating that husbands should love and serve their wives as Christ does the church because they are "one body with themselves." The wife is a man's own body. The sexual relationship within marriage actually makes two people become one, and that oneness has been given the holy role of representing the intimacy between Jesus Christ and His bride. Sex unites two people together in such a way that makes them one body and portrays the real presence of God.

I Corinthians 6:15-20 teaches us that our bodies are members of Christ himself and that we dare not take the members of Christ and unite them with a prostitute. When believers have sex with anyone other than their spouse, they become one with that person and are also uniting Christ with the other person. That's why this sin produces such grave consequences. In verses 18 and 19, Paul highlights the fact that sexual sin is a sin against the temple of the Holy Spirit. So when we have sex outside of marriage, we dishonor God with our bodies by becoming one in the wrong way.

Why Marriage?

Marriage is not for procreation only. Sexual union is for procreation (Genesis 1:28) but also for expressing love within the oneness of marriage *(Genesis 2:24; Proverbs 5:15-19; Corinthians &: 2-5)*. Although polygamy was practiced by some Old Testament personalities, monogamy was always God's ideal for humanity *(Mathews 19:4-5)*.

Many feel that if they don't want to have children, there is no need to be married. For singles, marriage should not be seen as just an act to keep from committing fornication. Before we get married, we are to know how to possess our vessel (body) in honor and purity.

> *I Thessalonians 4:3-4 -" It is God's will that you should be sanctified: that you should avoid sexual immorality; that each of you should learn to control his own body in a way that is holy and honorable." (NIV)*

Marriage is God's design for man and woman; it is His order for how things were to operate.

> *Genesis 2: 18, 22-25 The Lord God said, "It is not good for the man to be alone. I will make a helper suitable for him." ... Then the Lord God made a woman from the rib he had taken out of the man, and he brought her to the man. The man said, "This is now bone of my bones and flesh of my flesh; she shall be called 'woman', for she was taken out of man. For this reason, a man will leave his father and mother and be united to his wife, and they will become one flesh. The man and his wife were both naked, and they felt no shame." (NIV)*

There was no need to be ashamed because they were in the will of God. Marriage was the relationship God would use to accomplish His purpose. The writer of Hebrews confirms marriage was esteemed.

Hebrews 13:4 "Marriage should be honored by all, and the marriage bed kept pure, for God will judge the adulterer and all the sexually immoral." (NIV)

The principle of cause and effect applies here even to marriage; the cause that a man was to leave his father and mother was for "marriage," a union of a man with a woman. From this union, the effect would be fruitful reproduction, children after their kind the parents, a covenant partnership. The bond between a child and his parents was strong then. The only other relationship which would be as strong, would be marriage an unbreakable covenant. The marriage relationship would symbolize the relationship between Christ and His Church!

The only way that a girl was to leave her mother and father was to enter into a secure relationship with a husband, who would protect her as her father had loved and protected her. He would not be her father. He would be her mate, her companion, her lover and her covering under the mighty hand of God. Living in today's society, it seems hard to visualize this type of relationship.

If a young man lives with his parents until he decides to marry, people will say he's a mamma's boy. Not so! A young man of those times would have had a strong relationship with his father. His father would have nurtured him and taught the ways of the Lord (Yahweh) and the ways and responsibilities of a husband.

According to the *Holman Bible Dictionary*, the father was very significant, though he may have very well been the grandfather or great-grandfather. His responsibilities included begetting, instructing, disciplining, and nurturing. The father even had the power to destroy family members if they enticed him from his loyalty to God *(Deuteronomy 13:6-10). Abraham's offering up of Isaac exemplifies his power as the father (Genesis 22).*

But the father was also to be a loving example of the love of God to his family. Children would be able to understand a loving God by the example of their father. Even the divine mercy displayed in the New Testament was drawn by the compassion of the Old Testament figure of the father *(Psalm 103).*

When Satan wanted to destroy God's creation, he went viciously after fathers; making them pervert the power God gave them to have dominion over the earth and their home. When he runs them out of the home, leaving their family, Satan knew the long-term effects which we feel today. So many young men are creating children but are unable to be fathers knowing the one thing the children would need was a loving, compassionate, protecting father. Our daughters are having babies with men not ready, nor capable of being fathers in the true sense of the word.

Yet, I understand that most women don't set out on a journey to be tossed from one man to another like an Old Testament concubine slave just having babies, as was their job! But as women, we hope that we will find the right man. When it does not work out, we pull ourselves together and keep on looking, believing. It is good to have faith that you'll find him, but have Bible faith that will not allow yourself to be sampled.

If he is sent from God, he will appreciate and love me for whom God has made me and is continuing to make me. The intimacy so longed for, that the Lord desires is to be reserved for your King. The love and commitment from a Queen is for her God and her King, as in her husband. The concubine was secondary with no legal status, the Queen was the primary wife and had a say in how the concubine was treated.

It is extremely important for a woman to realize the necessity of having a mate who believes the word of God and the design for the family. The man is the head of the home. The type of head he will be will depend on the headship of Christ in his life. A godly man is worth waiting for accept nothing less. We are all lifelong projects for the Holy Spirit to transform into the image of Christ, but there should be some basis in the life of one being considered for partnership that the Lord has his heart. Otherwise, you will wind up like many women used, abused and left alone.

This is not God's plan for you. This is the enemy's plan. Your choice is to either settle for what Satan has to offer or wait on the Lord and be of good courage and He shall strengthen thine heart: wait I say on the Lord *(Psalms 27:14)*.

The woman who was caught in adultery was brought before Jesus (perhaps by some of the same men that had spent time with her) to make a public example of her. But Jesus understood this woman's pain. Perhaps, for the first time, this man, who was righteous and had the power and the right to judge, forgave her and told her go and sin no more (John 8:1-11). In the most sincere and gentle way, He didn't excuse her, He told her, yes; you did what they accused you of. But now, go and don't do these things again.

How many of us fell in love with Jesus because others accused us and condemned us without knowing our plight? But we heard Jesus say, go, change. Don't keep on the same path. I give you permission and power to change. Daughters, the Lord has so much more for us. At times, people have failed us, and we often feel lonely. But Jesus said go, and don't go the same way. Change!

When we change, you can feel his restoration and cleansing power that will rebuild your self-esteem and restore what the devil robbed from you. The Lord wanted her from that day on to start afresh, her past remitted. When a daughter makes up her mind to change because she wants to please God, things begin to happen.

Your focus will change. God will steer you in the right direction because now you want Him and will listen for His directions. His voice and desires become more important to you than your own. Your spirit will stand up and your flesh will be subject to the spirit's control. All this happens when God's spirit is allowed to guide you by your free will. There is a regal spirit in you and will be exposed after your awareness of who you are in Christ; an heir adopted into the family of God; a chosen generation of a royal priesthood!

Be the Queen you were meant to be and don't settle for the life of a concubine.

Marriage - A Sacred Covenant

From the beginning, God instituted marriage as a covenant relationship, which was sealed by a blood sacrifice. As Adam the first man had a bride, so Jesus the last Adam has a bride. The first Adam and his bride were covered through the shedding of blood of animal sacrifices and the second Adam, **JESUS CHRIST THE RIGHTEOUS,** shed His own blood for his bride to seal the covenant. Every covenant involved a blood sacrifice. The scriptures speak of four blood sacrifices.

The ***first*** took place in the Garden of Eden when God clothed Adam and Eve with coats of skins to shed blood by the substitution sacrifice of animals to cover their sins. God continues to have fellowship with man and appease His justice and guard His holiness. God's covenant to assure the redemption of man. For without the shedding of blood there is no remission of sin (Heb. 9:22). From then on, before Christ came, people showed repentance by the blood sacrifice of animals.

When God made His covenant *(the second)* with Abraham, He required blood through circumcision as an act of good faith on Abraham's part symbolizing by the cutting away of his foreskin that his heart had gone through a change (an outward show of an inward work). The ***third*** is the atoning blood of Jesus, God's covenant to us that if we confess our sins, He is willing to forgive us and cleanse us from all unrighteousness. There need be no more sacrifices for the blood of Jesus replaces the need for any more blood sacrifices for sin.

But there is another blood sacrifice that brings people into a covenant agreement with God. He still desires that we practice it. That is only by way of marriage and that is the sexual union of husband and wife. Notice we say husband and wife **in** marriage.

You might ask, how so? Under Hebrew marriage customs, when it came time for the marriage to be consummated, the groom escorted the bride to their new home, accompanied and met by celebrating friends of the two families *(Judges 14:12-18; Mathew 25:113)*. There, a wedding celebration took place that might last an entire week *(Genesis 29:27; Judges 14:12-18; John 2:1-11)*. During the festivities, the bride and groom dressed and were treated as king and queen.

The marriage was consummated during the festival week in the bride chamber, or huppa, while the guests waited outside. The parents of the bride would present them with white linens for their wedding night. They were expected to sleep on them, and the bride was expected to bleed on them as proof of her virginity. God created women with a protective membrane, the hymen, which in most cases is broken the first time any woman has intercourse. When it breaks, a woman's blood covenant between her and God is established.

The biblical concept of marriage, then, is that of a lifelong covenant relationship established between one man and one woman, which is to be nurtured by love and intimacy, enabling the couple to experience life in this world together and creating a healthy climate in which to bring up children. This covenant relationship is used by God to illustrate the depth of his own commitment to Israel *(Isaiah 62:4,5; Jeremiah 31:32)*.

Husbands are to love their wives as Christ loved the church and gave himself up for her *(Ephesians 5:25)*, while wives respond to their husbands' love by freely submitting *(Ephesians 21-24)*. Covenant commitment provides the framework for marriage, and this reality is experienced as husband and wife each respond with deepening love to the other.

The Old Testament describes other forms of marriage, specifically polygamy and concubinage, which do not match the ideal. In the context of their times, the relationship that Abraham established with Hagar *(Genesis 16)* and that of Jacob with Rachel and Leah *(Genesis 29)* were valid marriages, for that society judged it legitimate for them to live together, though their multiple marriages were out of the pattern that God intends for humanity. Similarly, the multiple marriages of Solomon, many of which were political in nature and were entered into as a way of ratifying treaties with other nations, were valid marriages from a sociological standpoint, even though in marrying as he did, Solomon directly violated God's command *(Deuteronomy 17:16-17)* and thus damaged his relationship with God.

God's marital ideal is intended to guard us from alternate forms of marriage that society may invent, forms that are ultimately harmful to human beings. We need only review the anguish that Abraham and Jacob experienced and the spiritual idolatry into which Solomon fell as a direct result of their multiple marriages to sense the destructive potential of alternate forms of marriage. The farther a society strays from the ideal presented in Scripture, the greater the social and personal dangers involved.

Pray this prayer,

Dear Heavenly Father,

Help me to see who I am in you, that I might recognize and become in conduct and lifestyle, the daughter you died and cleansed me to be. As a new creature in Christ help me to be aware of the power within me to live holy and righteous in this present world, and bring you glory and honor. Build within a hunger and thirst for your Word that I will read it and retain it in my heart that I might not sin against thee.

I present my body to you as a living sacrifice and confess that I am not my own, for I have been bought with a price-the precious blood of Jesus Christ, my Lord and my God! My body is the temple of the Living God and I reserve it for you and my covenant partner when and if you shall send him. Until that time,

I will commit my body with its emotions and will to you and your Word. I make your will more important than my will and ask for it to be done. In your strength I will wait on you patiently, and work to build up the kingdom of God and be a living witness for others of your love, mercy, and grace!

Love,

Your Daughter

Journal Page

(What Thoughts Did The Holy Spirit Give You In This Chapter)

"Marriage should be honored by all, and the marriage bed kept pure, for God will judge the adulterer and all the sexually immoral." Hebrews 13:4 (NIV)

CHAPTER THREE

"The Courtship"

The Courtship

> *"Flee the evil desires of youth, and pursue righteousness, faith, love, and peace, along with those who call on the Lord out of a pure heart." 2Tim. 2:22 (NIV)*

The purpose for dating is to determine the suitability of an individual for you. Is this person a suitable candidate to spend time getting to know? A time to see what he is really all about. Does what this person envisions for their future present balance for how you see yours. In other words, you use this time to collect information. So often this period for learning about each other's views, on subjects important to governing your relationship as husband and wife, is used to develop or determine physical attractions. Obviously, there is some attraction in order to contemplate dating. But this should not be promoted at this time. To involve the physical attraction before determining whether you are compatible in dating is putting the "cart before the horse".

> *I Thessalonians 4:3-4 "It is God's will that you should be sanctified: that you should avoid sexual immorality; that each of you should learn to control his own body in a way that is holy and honorable, not in passionate lust like the heathen, who do not know God; ..." (NIV Study Bible)*

Because no matter how much you may physically be attracted to each other, and yet have very little in common in other areas is not a prerequisite for a short-term courtship; and a long term for a broken heart and disappointment. As women we want the physical romance right away, not necessarily sexual, but cuddling, light kissing, and what might seem like innocent petting. But this leads us to stronger desires and weakens our guard, even before we know how long we will be with this person.

Our heart gets deeply involved and our actions follow. But we are to "guard our hearts with all diligence." These are the tactics the enemy uses to get a foothold in our desire to have someone.

There is no need to develop a great physical attraction for someone you don't really know. While you are dating, you should try to determine if this person were someone you would even consider discussing spending a lifetime relationship with. No man should be dated in a "holding pattern" (i.e. while you're waiting for someone you really want or like to come along). The questions and answers as to physical attraction are for the courtship period. If you both find each engaged in meaningful and stimulating conversation, that is a good start. Here are some things you should learn about the individual.

- Their spiritual position in Christ and level of maturity (you will see as time goes on, be observant)

- Family background, where raised

- Who raised them and how were they raised

- Type of relationship they have with family members

- Their educational level

- The goals for their future

These and other questions are important, because if you develop a relationship with this person, who has the potential to lead to marriage, you will have to take into account all of what this person brings with them. We all have issues, at least have a clue what the real issues are you will have to accept or reject dealing with.

Once you have established this information and desire in agreement with him truly knowing that each other's background may be different, seek to complement each other. Perhaps it is the time, with the understanding that this level is for serious marriage contenders, to determine if you both are spiritually, mentally, emotionally, and financially suitable. After this we can investigate the chemistry between both of you. There should and must be ground rules laid for the courtship period. The courtship is for those who are seeking marriage. The courtship means we have talked long enough to learn and know somewhat who this person is and what things we have in common. Our goals for the future in Christ are in agreement; intellectually (i.e. the way we think) we are compatible. Our views on the handling of finances along with its responsibilities are in agreement. We both believe in spiritual counseling. We believe in keeping debts low and savings high. We support working together as partners and find each other physically and mentally attractive. Both of us are looking for spousal potential in each other and think the possibility exists.

This is a time to be most prayerful and wise. You must maintain your integrity while being aware of the chemistry you both feel. Please pay particular attention to this chapter and don't feel you are too grown to receive advice from others. This is what the enemy relies on to use and have as an advantage. But continue to pray and seek God's will for you and for him in this relationship. The scriptures tell us in *Psalm 37:3 (NASB):*

> *"Trust in the Lord and do good; dwell in the land and enjoy safe Pasture. Delight yourself in the Lord and he will give you the desires of your heart."*

How About A Date

This subject is important for youth and adults alike. Dating is necessary and can be a wonderful time to assess the qualities and characteristics that are compatible with you. Dating is spending time with different persons you feel are potential candidates for a lifelong partnership. The goal is to learn about others as well as about you. For how does one know what is good for them when they don't always know themselves?

So, while you are learning about others, you will find out much about your own likes, dislikes, and how ready you are to share your life with another individual. Dating can really be fun when you do it God's way and with an understanding you won't necessarily find or be ready to come to any conclusions in a short period of time. Don't try to put any pressure on yourself by setting limits on how long it will take to agree with who will be a suitable mate.

I have stated that dating can be fun, depending on who you are dating and the character of that person. It would be good to know people who already know the person with whom you may be planning to give time.

It is important for all women young or old to know whom you are dating because your safety could be at stake. Besides this, they may not be the type of person who will respect your stand in Christ. This is a bad start. Don't be tricked by someone who dates you with the pretense he wants to know about your faith. Invite him to church, and Bible class. If he's really interested, he will go. You have to be so careful, for the devil is always looking to pull you out of the covering of the blood of Christ, where you are protected. He will appear as an angel of light and be a subtle snake.

I have seen more young ladies pulled out of the will of God by pretending men who said they wanted to be saved and it was only to get the woman they were pursuing. It was the chase that fascinated them. After the capture, they looked for the next challenge. A word of caution: don't say yes right away to any person because they received salvation while pursuing you. Wait and give God time to change the heart of your candidate of interest, and they begin to learn how to walk in the spirit and discern the voice of God. All of this will be necessary for a covenant partner relationship. So don't be afraid to give it time.

What should be the proper age to start dating? The parents should resolve that issue. This includes the terms of the dating process with clear instructions to their children with the advisement of your pastor through the Word of God.

I recommend for parents and single adults, an excellent book by *Josh McDowell, "Why True Love Waits" (Tyndale House Publishers/ Copyright 2002)* would be helpful and informative when discussing the matter of dating with your teens and young adults. But the rules at any age are basically the same on conduct. I believe it will be good to make notes and track experiences you will have on your dates.

Remember, dating is different from a courtship. Dating is to determine who is eligible for courtship. By the time you get to courtship, you both have determined that you are suitable, compatible, and attractive spiritually and naturally for each other.

Dating takes time. Don't rush it. Remember, the scriptures teach us to be anxious for nothing, but in all things prayerful and to make our requests known to God and trust Him and wait on **Him** to do what is best for you.

Allow me to recommend some practical advice on dating for your consideration.

- Keep your dates public. Be in an open surrounding and yet a quiet setting where you can talk and get to know one another. This is a time for collecting data (information) about this person. Pay attention closely because you don't want to plan a second date with someone you feel will not be right for you just for the sake of being polite. It will be more gracious to conclude the process without hurting the person and leading them on to believe there may be a chance this could develop into something you know will not.

- Before the date, prepare what will make for good conversation. Perhaps you can discuss that person's likes and their interests. During the conversation, be a good listener and at times, share your interests, goals and accomplishments without any signs of arrogance. Always give God the glory for the things He has done **in** your life.

- Plan what you will wear ahead of time. If he is making the plans and hasn't asked you for any suggestions on what you feel comfortable doing, find out where he is planning to take you. This will help you determine the appropriate attire for this occasion. Today's styles are pretty seductive. Make sure they do not overly influence you to project the wrong image of yourself. Remember, you represent Christ in all that you do. Pray about having the right spirit when selecting an outfit to wear. You can look very fashionable and feminine, which can be more attractive than the sexier outfits. Don't play up what you are not willing to give up!

- When you learn where you are going, always let someone know where you are going and whom you are going with. Carry a cell phone should plans change at the last minute. You can always discreetly inform someone of your changein plans and how they can reach you in an emergency.

- Become familiar with new standards in etiquette and table manners. Practice, if you feel awkward about eating out at one of the finer dinner restaurants where the place settings may be a little more elaborate. You are a Queen in training. David was a King in training. He didn't know how to go in or out of the palace, but God put him in a place of preparation. So don't be intimidated. This is just another step on your way to the palace.

- Have a set time to be home. Leave them wanting more time to see you, if you feel there is potential for a second date. Do try to assess the person's character and personality traits during this time. Once you have done that, determine whether it is conducive to go any further. Don't waste time dating just for the sake of saying I have a date. The purpose of dating is to collect information to help you determine if there is potential for furthering the relationship.

- If you sincerely pass the first three or four dates and see that there is a slight attraction and plan to continue seeing each other, some boundaries need to be worked out that you both should agree on as Christians. The purpose of Christians dating is to find a compatible mate for a marriage partner and not a longtime girlfriend. If you both are attracted to each other, the attraction will only grow stronger. What used to be exciting will progress to long stares and smiles, handholding, arms around the waist, and more intimate gestures.

- The reason for this, which Tim Alan Gardner writes in his book, *Sacred Sex (WaterBrook Press/ Copyright 2002)* is the **"law of diminishing returns."** "This law states that if the main focus is in deriving pleasure and physical gratification, then that pleasure will diminish with time. To receive the same level of pleasure enjoyed in the past will mean you have to increase the pleasure stimuli. This is the principle which operates in the life of drug addicts and can also be applied to the levels of intimacy in a courtship and sex in general as well." So you will both have to sit down as mature Christian adults and plan and pray how to keep the enemy of lust from steering this potential relationship off course.

- This will be made easier if you keep your courting public or in the presence of others always. If you both live alone, I don't suggest you entertain at either of your apartments, if there will be no other Christian couples present. And they should leave when you leave and stay while you are there. While this may seem like immature behavior, it is actually good Christian practice to defeat the devil's devices. The Bible says in *J Cor. 10:12* "Therefore let him who thinks he stands take heed that he does not fall."

- Having stated all this, keep in mind wherever you start to show affection when you move to a new level, it is hard to return to just what was done before that. For instance, hand holding and long glances in each other's eyes will definitely provoke kissing, which could start out innocently on the cheek or gently on the lips and progress to open mouth kissing. Once you move to this level, it is difficult to go back to just holding hands.

Before you know it, you will move to heavy petting while dressed and then what. I think you get the picture. There is nothing hidden from God, and you do want to please him even in your courtship.

- At this point, dating which has moved to courting cannot be endless. There should be planning for the wedding and preparation, not just for a ceremony but also for a life together. This planning should include counseling by the pastors of both your churches, if you are not attending the same church. You should both be of the same religious beliefs to avoid conflict.

- Pray together often and encourage each other through the Word of God, begin the lifelong practice now. Remember you are entering into a covenant relationship, unbreakable before God.

Be sure to yield to God's will when making decisions about dating.

Psalms 37:3-4 "Trust in the Lord and do good; dwell in the land and cultivate faithfulness. Delight yourself in the Lord; and He will give you the desires of your heart." (NASE)

Ecclesiastics 12:1 "Remember also your creator in the days of your Youth, before the evil days come and the years Draw near when you will say, "I have no delight in them" ... (NASE)

Don't think yourself too old to receive sound instruction and advice from adults who love the Lord and try to exemplify Him in their walk.

Proverbs 1:8-9 "Hear, my son, your father's instruction and do not forsake your mother's teaching; indeed, they are a graceful wreath to your head and ornaments about your neck." (NASB)

Proverbs 5:1-2 "My son give attention to my wisdom, incline your ear to my understanding; that you may observe discretion and your lips may reserve knowledge." (NASB)

Keep your standard high and stay within biblical guidelines.

1 Tim. 4:12 "Let no one look down on your youthfulness, but rather in speech, conduct, love, faith and purity, show yourself an example of those who believe." (NASB)

1 Tim. 2:22 "Now flee from youthful lusts and pursue righteousness, faith, love and peace, with those who call on the Lord from a pure heart." (NASB)

Job 31:1 "I have made a covenant with my eyes, how then could I gaze at a virgin?" (NASB)

Job here shows the positive purpose of attesting loyalty to God as his sovereign Lord. Our behavior testifies of our loyalty to our Savior, and we must show our loyalty in all that we do, even how we date.

How About The Courtship?

1 Corinthians 6:9,11 "Know ye not that the unrighteous shall not inherit the kingdom of God? Be not deceived: neither fornicators, nor idolaters, nor adulterers, nor effeminate, nor abusers of themselves with mankind (men)..."

vs. 11 And such were some of you: but ye are washed, but ye are sanctified, but ye are justified in the name of the Lord Jesus, and by (in) the Spirit of our God. (Dickson NASE)

Know what you want and know yourself. Then you know what to seek for in prayer. Seek someone who will complement what you are not and who will be strong where you are weak. When a saved woman accepts a dinner or lunch invitation, it is a date where you are collecting data, information about his potential or the lack of it. The first pre-requisite is his spiritual position. But after that has been established, you must move on to see his strengths and weaknesses. While he is saved and loves the Lord, that is not enough alone to render him a good husband. It is only the starting point!

It is necessary to know if he has a job and how long he has been on this job. This can be a good indication of his employment stability and perhaps his income level (without asking directly). Answers are needed that discreetly can be ascertained over a period of time, the shorter the time the better. The amount and type of credit debt assumed is important. By the way, you want to make sure your debts are kept low. No man wants to assume a lot of debt going into marriage. If this is your problem, perhaps the Lord hasn't sent anyone because he wants to clear this matter up.

It is good to observe how he treats any female relations, which will display his attitude toward women. Even if he's saved, don't overlook this point! It is better to make it clear in the beginning of a courtship very sincerely and warmly that you are remaining celibate until marriage. This should be true even if you were sexually active prior to the now renewed commitment to refrain. If you had been sexually active in the past, you are now taking a stand. Just because you are not a virgin with an unbroken hymen, you can still be a virgin spiritually by abstaining from sexual sins. Sex is only a sin when performed outside of marriage.

The enemy will always make you feel like you have had sex with others, so what's the difference now. The difference is, as the light of understanding appears, walk in it. You must put aside the lusts of your flesh. You must stop doing what you know is displeasing to God and weakening your testimony of Christ to others. A good motivation is that anyone who truly wants to inherit the kingdom of God will not fornicate or commit adultery without repentance and a change of heart.

Don't Give Away Your Flavor

Most people like ice cream alone or with dessert. The variety reflected with so many flavors offers endless choices. While all flavors taste good, we all have our favorites. You have your own special flavor, which is perhaps to you better than the others, but there is no need to let anyone sample it before time. Certain flavors have to be appreciated over time. Revealing one before the mixture is finished is unfair to the creator. The time for tasting will come when the flavor is thoroughly refined and ready for tasting. For you, that day will be the night to seal the covenant. Some people like dessert before dinner, but the meal is the fortifying factor from which you get the greater nourishment and strength for your body. This same principal applies to your relationship to grow strong, trusting, honorable and glorifying before God. If you allow the entrance of strong passion with much kissing (mouth to mouth/French kisses) combined with hugging and close body contact, these things will be like quicksand, pulling you and leading you closer to breaking your will. Possibly, the relationship you are trying to build will be doomed. Obedience to God's Word is for your well-being and protection. The devil knows what it takes to get you for your wellbeing and protection. The devil knows what it takes to get you both to a place where you will for a moment drop your guard.

Be sober-minded, for the devil goes about as a roaring lion seeking whom he may devour. Passion is very intoxicating for a Christian, especially because it's off limits, just as the fruit was to Eve. But remember how they felt after they both partook of the fruit. Their eyes became open, and they were ashamed of their nakedness. You too will be ashamed of your disobedient act after the flesh has been gratified. Don't try to justify it by saying I'm engaged, so it's o.k. Wrong! Allow a period of innocence to be captured in the relationship even if you had previously been very free with intimacy. Satan wants you to lose that innocent feeling that you get back when you abstain from sexual intimacy.

The stage you started out in before sexual intercourse was one of innocence. There was no knowledge of a partner's desires, discovering comes as you explore each other's sensitive zones. This is always to be reserved for a covenant relationship.

All covenants were sealed by a blood sacrifice and marriage is a covenant, which would seal two people together by blood. As stated previously, the first act of sexual intercourse between a husband and wife would be sealed by the blood produced from the woman upon penetration of the male's penis. The act would break, tear or cut that tissue (the hymen) which covers the entrance to the female vagina, causing blood to flow over the male organ and uniting the two as one into an irrevocable covenant broken only by death. Both partners understood God's law. The first sexual act between a man and wife is to a sealing of the covenant relationship. Any believer, who is having a courtship and abstaining from any sexual acts regardless of the past, can regain a spiritual secondary virginity. You don't want to lose that for one moment of gratification with a possible lifetime of condemnation. If a couple that has committed themselves to the Lord is living together, they should make ways to live apart until the marriage ceremony to show their true love to God and for each other. Though there is forgiveness and grace, the self condemnation and scars will require much prayer and fasting to sometimes feel forgiven. Don't cheat yourself of the wonderful spiritual and natural passion of anticipation of becoming one with your partner and having God sanctify your union!!

Bad Company In The Church

1 Corinthians 5:9-11 (IAB) "When I wrote to you before, I told you not to associate with people who indulge in sexual sin. But I wasn't talking about unbelievers who indulge in sexual sin, or who are greedy or even swindlers or idol worshipers. You would have to leave this world to avoid people like that. What I meant was that you are not to associate with anyone who claims to be a Christian yet indulges in sexual sin, or is greedy, or worships idols, or is abusive, or a drunkard, or a swindler. Don't even eat with such people."

Paul makes it clear that we should not disassociate ourselves from unbelievers otherwise we could not carry out Christ's command to tell them about salvation. But we are to distance ourselves from the person who claims to be a Christian yet indulges in sins explicitly forbidden in Scripture by rationalizing his or her actions. By rationalizing sin, a person harms others for whom Christ died and dims God's "light" in himself or herself.

It is a matter of fact that those who are in Christ are new creatures with a totally new perspective. The old human perspective has passed away; behold, the new divine perspective has come and it's continuing to come. The Greek word "gegonen" perfect tense verb "has come" with a continuing action. The new creation with the new, divine perspective is a continual, growing ever-expanding experience. It is the experience of being changed into the likeness of Christ from one degree of glory to another *(2 Corinthians 3:18)* by beholding the glory of the Lord. Be ye transformed by the renewing of your mind. Not conformed to this world but transformed a new perspective.

Paul tells us again and again that we become the servant to whomever we obey. When we were sinners, we obeyed sin. But now grace has set us free from the law of sin and death. Free not to go on sinning, but to choose the other path of righteousness. Do not give yourself to unrighteousness, but instead give yourself completely to God since you have been given a new life. **Sin** is no longer your master, instead you are free by God's grace.

It is impossible to be neutral; every person has a master either God or Satan (sin). A Christian is not someone who cannot sin but someone who is no longer a slave to sin. He or she belongs to God. You are free to choose between two masters, sin (Satan) or righteousness and holiness (Jesus Christ). The Bible tells us that the wages of sin is death (spiritual and sometimes physical); but the gift of God is eternal life.

Weak Christians don't necessarily need to keep company together unless more stable Christians lead them. There is an old adage that says, "Association brings on assimilation." In other words, if you hang around certain types you often take on those same characteristics. It is the strong who are to bear the infirmities of the weak, not other weak persons!

So often, you get weak counsel because you ask weak saints for their opinions. A mature saint will say what you don't want to hear which is what the word of God says and means. Your flesh won't like it, but your spirit will rejoice.

Don't Go There!

> *1 Corinthians 6:15-17(LASB) "Don't you realize that your bodies are actually parts of Christ? Should a man take his body, which belongs to Christ, and join it to a prostitute? Never! And don't you know that if a man joins himself to a prostitute, he becomes one body with her? For the scriptures say, 'The two are united as one.' But the person who is joined to the Lord becomes one spirit with him."*

There are places you would never invite the visible Christ to go with you.

*By the way, any place not fit for you to invite **Him** is not fit for you to be either.*

Paul instructs the Corinthian church that we in fact take the invisible Christ places we don't really believe he's been. He told us that our bodies are the temples of the Holy Spirit. Because His spirit abides **in** us wherever we go in body, we bring Christ into the place, situation, or circumstance with us godly or ungodly.

So understanding this, we are to be particular about what we do with and to our bodies. We are one with Christ. In verse 18, he tells us to run away from sexual sin. This sin clearly affects the body because sexual immorality is a sin against your own body. This sin hurts God because it shows Him, we prefer following our own desires instead of the leading of the Holy Spirit.

Let Sleeping Dogs Lie

I believe this statement means to not wake up what could become a problem for you. The scriptures sometimes ask rhetorical questions such as:

Proverbs 6:27 "Can a man take fire in his bosom and His clothes not be burned?" (NASB)

Solomon was teaching something about lust that when it is unleashed, it is almost impossible to tame except for the grace and help from the Lord. Passions, which are aroused and experienced before marriage, are difficult to keep under control when placed in vulnerable situations. Notice I said difficult, not impossible! We cannot feed our passions when we are not in the right relationship to satisfy them. The only relationship acceptable to God is marriage. Marriage was created to allow two partners, husband and wife, male and female, to share the passion of this holy sacred union. There are steps we can take to help diminish the awakening of our passion.

- Avoid watching movies that create lustful mental pictures.

- Avoid conversations loaded with sexual innuendos.

- Avoid reading materials that arouse sexual mental images

- Avoid situations that can initiate compromising temporary pleasure.

- Avoid lustful soap operas that encourage your involvement in the characters and have led to the ruination of many women's character that actualized at night what they saw in the daytime dramas.

Words have so much power, whether spoken or read. Read Song of Solomon and see all the conversation of the two lovers throughout, which sounds very passionate. The language used is said to be an eschatological picture of Christ's union with the Church and marriage is also a model of the Church and Christ, the joy of the two becoming one. The power of life and death are in the tongue, spiritually as well as naturally. It was manifested in a negative way when the 1-900 numbers for phone sex came out. The response was overwhelming.

Now, we have the Internet and chat rooms where you can type in messages and get rapid responses, along with provocatively graphic pictures. Oh, the devil is trying to keep people trapped. Believe it or not, some of them are bible-believing Christians who have given in to the flesh. We can't give any space or opportunity to Satan's tactics to keep people in bondage. There are biblically based ways to obtain strength to resist the devil.

One such way is fasting, which can help starve your fleshly appetite for sin. It is a way of bringing down the strongholds of your flesh, for while it weakens the flesh, it strengthens the spirit. That is, if you are seeking God through prayer and meditating on His word.

> *Is. 58:6 "Is not this the fast that I have chosen? To loose the bands of wickedness, to undo the heavy burdens, and to let the oppressed go free, and that ye break every yoke?" (Dickson **NASB**)*

In this verse, God revealed through the prophet Isaiah that this fast was to break oppression and bondage and bring liberation. That is what fasting will do for us spiritually: it will break the bands of the wicked one in our lives. There are many books on fasting. I have often used Arthur Wallis's, *"GOD'S CHOSEN FAST"* as a guide and encouragement. Many times, when I needed a major breakthrough while battling my flesh, I turned to fasting and prayer.

The saying today, "Keep it Real," is the healthy type of relationship to have with God. Always confess to Him what exactly is going on with you in your secret closet of prayer, He will not be intimidated or blush over your honest assessments of how you are feeling often weakened. Ask him to strengthen you before you get into any situations. Ask your father and your savior and Lord to give you wisdom and integrity in your conduct. You want to be worthy of notice to those you are around and those you may be dating. Whatever your behavior has been in the past, it can and will be changed if you seek the Lord with a deep desire to change. Don't be afraid He will not fail you. The chapter on dating should help you formulate the dos and don'ts for your dates and take the steps to walk upright before God. Wait patiently for your desire and see what God will do.

Which Magazine Did You Read?

Almost every month, the cover of at least one leading mainstream magazine will feature an article title dealing with male and female relationships. Those articles basically deal with topics like: what a man wants, how to please your man, what men want from a relationship, how to get him to propose, or why he won't marry you.

But in December of 2003, one article listed the number one sin in dating, which was "sex too soon." The cover titled this observation, and I thought that while that sounded good, it needed to go a step further. It should have said the number one dating sin is sex before marriage! Sex before marriage assures nothing as pertaining to marriage.

Another article stated, as an advisory, that after you have dated for a period of time and you both feel comfortable and desire to take your relationship to the next level, you should exchange HIV testing results to each other in order to ensure safe sex. What craziness! As if that truly ensures you of safety. There are many STD's that you better be fearful of besides HIV; like the HPV virus, you can learn more about this in the chapter, What You Don't Know Can Hurt You. Also, read the story, *The Bite of the Vampire, chapter six.*

Most of the magazine articles take surveys of men and women and come off with findings that may temporarily help some women, but they mislead most. While this acknowledgement was good, it is not enough. How soon is too soon, ask the women with broken hearts, those who have contracted sicknesses and disease and those who have given of their youth, strength, dreams, hopes, commitment, loyalty and afterwards been traded in for someone new who would not allow themselves to be sampled until after the vows. Some women still believe that they are worthy and good enough to wait for. When you believe that about yourself you will radiate that to all those around you until it becomes infectious. Most men who are confident want someone who is confident as well. Often, we see ourselves according to the environment, family background, or negative perceptions of others and begin to identify ourselves in these images. Jesus was born of poor parents, but he didn't have a poverty mentality. He was not identified as the biological son of Joseph and was referred to as a bastard, but He knew who his father really was. And when we are born again, we too must see ourselves in light of who we are in Christ!

We cannot allow magazine articles to influence us in our conduct for the Word of God gives life and it gives direction on how to live "holy" in this present world.

Galatians 1:4 (Dickson NASR) "Who gave himself for our sins, that He might deliver us from this present evil world, according to the will of God and our Father."

The best that the world has to offer women in these times is to settle for being a man's concubine. His property to use and discard if you are not pretty enough, if you are not pleasing enough or long enough in order to win him over. You must have the right performance and after enough tricks, you might catch him. He should be trying to catch you, because you are God's gift to man.

Any woman, who has made up her mind to follow Christ, and do it His way, must seek to keep herself undefiled and pure until God directs her covenant partner to her, who will appreciate what the Lord has prepared for him. You will be God's gift to him. While you're waiting for God's man, use the time to prepare yourself for marriage by building first your relationship with the Lord. Your communication with him in your singleness will be a great factor in your communication with him in your married life. Here are a few suggestions.

- Spend time building up the arsenal of the Word of God in your heart, which is the sword of the spirit for the times the enemy will come up against your marriage, your family, and your finances.

- Learn how to apply the word to your current vicissitudes of life.

- Learn how to hear the voice of God for direction in and for every area of your life. You will need to do all of this and more for spiritual warfare.

- Establish goals, which can work during your singleness, and benefit you also in marriage.

- Before you get married, read books that pertain to marriage counseling and be mature about many of the problems, which confront married couples especially Christian marriages.

The scriptures teach us:

> *"so that no advantage would be taken of us by Satan, for we are not ignorant of his scheme." 2 Corinthians 2:11 (NASB)*

Remember nurturing your relationship with Christ will nurture your relationship with your covenant partner. As a helpmeet, you will truly need to be sensitive to the Holy Spirit's leading. So, what better time to start making this principle practical in your walk with the Lord than now!!!

Let's pray, Heavenly Father,

I thank you for the privilege to come to your throne of Grace boldly and make my requests known to you. I ask you to help me be the living epistle, which all men can look upon and see you operating in my life. You have blessed me with all spiritual blessings in the heavenlies through Jesus Christ my Lord and Savior. Therefore, I have the power to wage war against and win the warfare against my enemy Satan and his spiritual wicked forces.

Let your Word uphold me, let your Holy Spirit quicken me and keep me alert to all of his devices and help my faith to trust in you despite what I see, and speak those things that be not as though they were. I take control over my flesh through your spirit, which abides in me and brings it under subjection to your will and your Word.

Love,

Your Daughter

Journal Page

(What Thoughts Did The Holy Spirit Give You In This Chapter)

"Rather, clothe yourselves with the Lord Jesus Christ, and do not Think about how to gratify the desires of the sinful nature." (Romans 13:14 NIV)

CHAPTER FOUR

Your Choice in Men

Your Choice In Men

Most women have a wish list of qualities they want in a man, or at least the man they desire to marry. We look for certain things in men, but often the search is too superficial. You have the right to want certain physical qualities, but don't obsess over them. Be flexible in this area. Judge the inward qualities first and then the external. What we look for has to do with what we have or have not had.

As mentioned previously, I made the wrong choices at times and regretted it. What I was looking for was not the composite for a husband but was more like a father. You may want to marry someone with or without qualities like your father. But you do not want to marry someone who will act like your father.

You should have sound reasoning for what you want in an individual. You should compare what you want to the scriptures. He should believe that the Bible is the true Word of God and that it should govern the lives of believers! The Bible should be the source to settle disputes and have the final say for the husband and wife despite their personal thoughts. After all, we are to let the Word of God be true and every man a liar. Man's word has no strength, against what God says to us through His scriptures. If a man will listen to God, then when you can't get him to hear you, you can pray and God can talk to him.

This chapter is not to tell you what to like, but rather what you will want to consider, as you determine the type of person you will ultimately marry and start a family. Pray and ask God to make your God-given man **in** His image, with a heart for God. Someone who is strong to cover his wife and family with prayer always, someone who will rush to the throne of God in the face of immediate danger to his wife or his family. A man who will do as the scriptures say, *"Husbands, love your* wives, just as Christ also loved the church and gave Himself for it" (Ephesians 5:25). The **NASB** footnote tells us this about this scripture's meaning:

"Paul now shows that this is not a one-sided submission, but a reciprocal relationship. Love is explained by what follows. Gave Himself up for her. Not only the expression of our Lord's love, but also an example of how the husband ought to devote himself to his wife's good. To give oneself up to death for the beloved is a more extreme expression of devotion than the wife is called on to make."

The Bible outlines what a man should be and how a woman ought to respond to such a mate. God's standards are high. Therefore, we should not feel that we have to lower them to accomplish His desire for His daughters. Remember to go beyond superficiality. Don't only look at his outward appearance. It is all right to have a realistic wish list.

You can make your requests known unto God. But don't get stuck on looks alone, when most of the other essential qualities are present. Check out his spirit and heart. These are two attributes that God will have to reveal to you. Choose what God would choose for you, only the best in spirit!

Rahab Got A Good Man

"And Salmon begat Boaz of Rahab; and Boaz beget Obed of Ruth; and Obed begat Jesse..." Mathew 1:5 (Dickson NASB)

A harlot marries one of the princes of Israel, who was also one of the men that Joshua sent to spy out the city of Jericho. This woman's faith in the God of Israel brought her a greater blessing. Not only did she save her family from destruction and wrath, but also, they were placed in a position to know first-hand the GOD of Israel! She married into a distinguished family of Israel of the tribe of Judah the lineage of our LORD JESUS CHRIST!

What is interesting about this story is that it teaches us further about the love of God toward those who love, believe, and reverence Him. If any of us had known Salmon, we would never have hooked him up with Rahab. Those of us who believe in strict holiness would have said he should be with a virgin, a woman with a spotless reputation, a woman who had no children, of good parentage. He would never have been introduced to a woman of such background. Surely, she would not rate a man like this. But when God sanctifies you, when he sees your faith, your heart, and He cleanses you, He prepares you to receive his best. Man, usually looks on the outward appearance, but God looks on the heart!

Many daughters in God's house who have been "born again" should not think of themselves as undeserving of such a man as Salmon. And no man should look at a woman's past and count her out as unfit or less than worthy. But for the GRACE OF GOD, there goes anyone of us. Given Rahab's situation, circumstance, or family dysfunction, who knows where the best of us would be? Who knows if someone had not helped you or turned you around, where you would be today? The scriptures tell us that no man ought to think more highly of himself than he ought. They also tell us that he that thinketh he standeth take heed less he fall *(1 Corinthians 10: **12**).* For you don't know what you could have been or where you could find yourself in the future.

So every daughter should be encouraged to hold out for God's good man. A man who will love you and your family, your children, if there be any. Don't think that because you have had a divorce or child out of wedlock or numerous relationships that failed, that you don't deserve God's best. The devil always tries to make you feel like you can't have the best because you are not perfect enough. In all actuality, who is? All have come short of the glory of God, even after being born again, of the water and spirit, and speaking with other tongues as the spirit of God gives utterance! We're striving to die daily (or we should be) and we need the Lord's help. Don't compromise or settle for anyone less than God's best.

God's best is not only a man or woman with a sizeable income, substantial bank account, polished demeanor and dress or commendable education. These are assets to any marital relationship. However, in and of themselves, without compassion and a sincere heart for God and His word, they hold little value. If you had all of them and did not have a man after God's own heart, you will find that he will never love you properly. He has to love God and believe His word is the first and foremost guide for every area of his life. Both parties must agree that the LORD and His Word will rule their lives together.

Perhaps, Rahab was never looking for more than just saving her life and her family because she believed on the God of Israel. If any woman, girl, or person will believe that God's way is the only way and do it like He says, I believe that eyes have not seen and ears have not heard, neither has it entered into your heart the things that God has (already) prepared for them that love Him. Love **Him** enough to obey **Him** at all costs.

Wait on the Lord and be of good courage, despite the loneliness, again I say, wait on the Lord. If many women in the church would be honest, they would tell you about the consequences of not waiting on the Lord.

Jacob Is No Candidate -Yet

Jacob was the second son of Isaac and Rebecca and twin brother of Esau. He was good and yet he was bad. He had many inconsistencies in his life. He was a product or victim of his mother's partiality *(Genesis 25:28);* "Rebekah loved Jacob", is emphasized as if she loved Esau less. **He** was selfish, for when his brother came in from the field faint with hunger, Jacob used his brother's hunger as a bargaining tool to get what he wanted from him. His mother prompted this.

Jacob was naturally crafty and deceitful without his mother's aid. But she helped to promote his actions rather than train him to resist them. Jacob cheated *(Genesis 25:29-34),* deceived *(Genesis 27:1-29),* had to flee for his life *(Genesis 27:43, 28:1-5),* rose to a higher level *(Genesis 28:10-22)* had a romance spoiled and reaped some of the seeds he had himself planted (Genesis 29:15-30), was affectionate *(Genesis 29:18)* **He** was prayerful *(Genesis 32:9-12, 24-30),* he was given a divine call to the promised land *(Genesis 31)* was disciplined by God through affliction *(Genesis 37:28; 42:36),* he was a man of faith *(Hebrew 11:21).*

The contradiction of Jacob's nature is true for more men who are being brought into a new closer walk with God, when God is trying to change their hearts.

When a daughter of God is seeking a mate, she must decide what spiritual stage Jacob is at in his transition. You can be so anxious for him to be saved and filled with the spirit of God that you don't let God complete the renewal process in him. You interfere with the work He is doing **in** that man's life. A lot of baggage and old ways (old nature) must change. God may have to wrestle with him and break him until his heart is changed toward Him first, never mind you right now!

For if God is unable to get his heart, you will never have it safely. If God does not make him a son because of his own willingness to receive Christ as his Lord and Savior (John 1:12), he will not come to know his Heavenly Father's love as a son. He needs to know that his true father has always loved him (for whom the Lord loveth he chaseneth). If not, you will be dealing with that inconsistent, confused son, who doesn't really know "what love has to do with it!" When God finishes the work, his name will be changed from Jacob (trickster/deceiver) to Israel (ruleth with God).

You Can't Change Jacob

Many women think that they can change a man. You may be able to impact his life, you can be an example and a light to him; but change him you cannot. The heart is a place for the Holy Spirit to work. That man must cry Abba, Father before he can truly consider giving his heart to you *(Romans 8:15-16)*. Let's be honest. You couldn't change your own heart. You don't even know all the secrets **in** your heart *(Jeremiah 17:9-10, Hebrew 4:12)*. Only God knows the heart through and through.

He may have to chastise Jacob. He may have to afflict him to create a tender heart and change its intents. But whatever God has to do, let Him do it. The Lord is the only one who has full information about him and who will chastise him in His love. You may think he needs your kind of love. And in part, he does but not yet. **He** is on the verge of becoming "Israel." Don't interfere with the process. All God had to do is begin the work. If he started it, He will surely finish it!

Judging His Spirit

When you choose to partner with a man you are actually partnering with his spirit. His spirit will govern him and if the Holy Spirit does not guide him, he is not even a ready candidate for marriage. Moses could take Joshua at God's direction because God said he was, "a man in who is the spirit" *(Numbers 27:18)*. Of Isaiah God said, "I have put my spirit upon him" *(Isaiah 42:1)*. The Lord can direct a man who has his spirit, for they that worship God must do so in "spirit and in truth."

You cannot be deceived by his biceps, triceps, hair, face, or any other superficial advantage for the "grass fadeth and the flower withereth." Time will take away some of the outward things we emphasize. There's nothing wrong with desiring an attractive mate, but don't let that be the main appeal. Get to know the spirit of the individual. It is his spirit that you will be asked to be submissive to, "... so let the wives be to their own husbands in everything" *(Ephesians 5:24)*.

It is okay to say, "I'm entertaining you to judge whether you are a potential candidate for a husband." This sets the tone for the relationship, which is always to be conducted in a public arena. After all, you don't need a boyfriend, you want a covenant partner!

Sister To Sister

We read about the conflict of Esau and Jacob, which was the result of Jacob's tricking his brother Esau out of his birthright or blessing. The first time was because Esau valued his appetite more than his blessing *(Genesis 25:29-34)*.

Before we criticize Esau, this is a good time to look at how little we value our promised blessings from God. We give them up so easily to gratify our flesh. It does not always have to be in a sexual way. But the lust for things can cause us to lose our birthright, our inherited blessings. The second time was because Jacob conspired with his mother, Rebekah to get the blessing, which was meant for the elder son.

Isaac sent Jacob away to Paddan-aram *(Gen. 28:2)* to find a wife in his uncle Laban's house. Laban was Rebekah's brother. When Jacob met Laban, he met his match. Laban had two daughters: Leah was the eldest and Rachel was the youngest. Jacob met Rachel and immediately fell in love. According to the scriptures, Rachel was the prettier of the two (Leah was not mentioned as being beautiful). It was noted that she was not beautiful in comparison to Rachel. Jacob went to Laban, her father, and asked for her hand in marriage. Laban agreed, but he would have to work seven years for him to acquire her. Jacob agreed. It is said that those seven years was as seven days to him because he loved her so much.

Allow me to make a point here. Many times, a woman wants to know how she can be certain if a man loves her or not. This is a great example of a man's love for a woman. A woman he probably had never kissed, perhaps never held her hand, and certainly never had any kind of sexual relations with her. Yet, this young man was willing to work seven years to get her. He had a promise that after the seven years, he would be able to have her.

I believe that the absence of intimacy made him want her the more. His anticipation of what it would be like was a constant motivation for him. Just the thought of having her excited him. To want her and not be able to have her, but to have a promise that if he did what her father said, he would have her. As time passed, he was so in love with her that the time passed so rapidly.

I believe that this type of feeling for a man is so precious and euphoric that when a woman gives in before their time, it robs him of this excitement. Because it can only happen if you refuse to give in to his flesh or his passionate desire to have you. While it may at first anger him and even at times frustrate him, it also excites him. This is also why you must keep your times together, public and chaperoned.

This is what makes the honeymoon night so special, you two have waited. Now, because you have done what your Father asked you to do, you can experience unashamedly (Heb. 13:4), the mystical union of becoming one flesh; as God designed for those in a covenant relationship. So, don't give in before the covenant is sealed. We want to have someone tell us they love us so desperately that when a man says he does, we feel we have him. Well, it's not what he says as much as what he does.

Jacob proved his love for Rachel. When it was time for the wedding, the celebration lasted about seven days *(Genesis 29:22,27-28; Judges 14:10,12)* and on the night of the wedding, Laban brought his daughter in customary attire veiled and unrecognizable *(Genesis 29:23-25)*. That night, Jacob went **in** to her and consummated the marriage. That act sealed the covenant, which made it irreversible. So, the next morning, he arose only to find out that he was not with Rachel, but with her elder sister Leah. He was furious with Laban and disappointed.

When he approached Laban over what had been done by switching sisters, Laban said that it was customary for the older sister to marry first. In other words, Laban assumed Jacob knew the custom after abiding in the land for seven years. While

Laban knew that Jacob probably didn't know the customs of that city or peoples, he may have felt it was his responsibility to ask and know. So he took advantage of what he didn't know. Doesn't this sound familiar? The devil takes advantage of what you don't know. If you don't know that God will bless you if you will do things like His word says to do it, you will become a victim of your own ignorance.

Laban told Jacob about the law. After a week, Laban told Jacob he could have Rachel. But Jacob would have to agree to work another seven years. Leah knew what was going on but was obedient to her father. She knew Jacob didn't love her, but she knew that her future was insured. Now Jacob could blame no one but himself for not knowing the rules of the place he resided. He should have investigated things a little further. He didn't know the consequences for being ignorant to these customs or laws. This is how some of us operate in the kingdom of God. We don't know when we ask God for something, we should understand the principles of the kingdom and how God operates. So when we make our requests known, we know God does everything in decency and in order. We should know that we are to seek him first and be obedient. We are to be holy. So that when we pray, we pray for His will to be done.

Jacob got Rachel but on condition that he had to work an additional seven years for her father, Laban. He only wanted one woman. Now, he has two plus their handmaidens, for a total of four women. He also got the one who would be his primary wife, who was not the prettiest *(Genesis 29:17)*. Leah's name meant cow and Rachel's name meant ewe as in a lamb. You can draw from the association of their names, why Jacob favored Rachel over Leah. So his primary wife in this case, was the one who was not the prettiest. She was the one he would not have desired, but this one was blessed first because she did exactly what her father told her to do. What Laban did was legal in his land and part of the rule of his peoples.

When Jacob asked for Rachel, he was saying I'd marry Leah first in order to have Rachel (according to the law of the land the elder sister must be married first). So, Jacob could acquire Rachel, but only by first marrying Leah. He just didn't know it because he didn't know the principles by which the land he resided in operated. Well, we will be blessed if we know the rules of the kingdom where we dwell. Our Heavenly Father will bless us and secure a future for us with many blessings, if we do what He says do. Be obedient to His Word.

Leah was so blessed that she was able to bear six sons for Jacob while Rachel only had two sons. God had chosen Leah to bare the son, Judah through whom the bloodline of the Messiah would come. She was not happy that her husband did not love her, and she had to watch him go to Rachel in love, while it was a chore for him to be with her. Rachel was blessed because she didn't ask for this situation. God knew the hearts of these women.

Rachel still served the gods of her father, for when it was time for them to leave, she stole the idols *(Genesis 31:19)* and hid them to ensure a safe journey. They were the gods of her father. They were so important to Laban that he chased them down to seek their return. But Rachel hid them because she did not trust in Jacob's God alone. While Rachel was beautiful on the outside, God was more pleased with what he saw in Leah. So your blessings are not determined by your hips, lips, or fingertips but by God. God can send you someone; no matter how you may think you look. So what you are not the most beautiful girl on campus, but you are godly, have integrity, and love the Lord with your whole heart. He will give you the desires of your whole heart. God will bless you so, that people will ask, how did she get him? Then you can say, God did it: it truly was the Lord.

The Conflict

There was a conflict between the two sisters, Leah and Rachel. God can bless you and someone is going to be mad if you get blessed. It just might be a family member; it just might be your sister. But don't let a man divide you and your sister. On the other hand, don't let your sister divide you and your husband, unless she has some truth to share with you about him. Maybe you were not the prettiest or the most likely to succeed. God can still bless you.

Leah and Rachel each had a handmaid, Zilpah and Bilhah, given to them as wedding gifts by their father. The sisters began competing with each other for Jacob's attention by bearing sons to him. And each of the two concubines had been given to Jacob. Polygamy is not for God's people. Daughters of the Most High only have to wait on Him and He will bring it to pass.

Philippians 4:6 "Be anxious for nothing, but in everything by prayer and supplication with thanksgiving let your requests be made known unto God." (NASR)

This resulted in future conflicts among the offspring. There was rivalry between *(Genesis 29:24,29; 30:3,9)* the brothers: divisions, envies, strife and even murder. Leah's sons tried to get rid of Joseph and sold him to traders on their way to Egypt *(Genesis 37:38)*. In later years, the Joseph tribes (especially Ephraim) and Judah competed for leadership. After Solomon's reign, the kingdom split in half. This all happened because a father showed partiality to one woman's children over the other. All of this because two sisters were rivals over one man. The younger sister should have known the rules.

What Jacob sowed in his earlier years was reaped in years following. But being a son of Abraham and having a promise to be fulfilled through him, he was blessed. Jacob had an encounter with God where he "struggles with God" *(Genesis 32:28)* and was changed by it. Once a deceiver who had used all kinds of schemes and tactics to achieve his own goals, he now submitted to God and the life changing experience followed. Jacob's name was changed to Israel, and he received God's blessings.

A little note here: when a man is wrestling with God, wait until the struggling is over and the full change has come, before you try to change him and before you commit to him.

The Flavor of Favor

The book of Esther is a very popular account of a woman who put her life on the line for her people, and said, *"if I perish, I perish but I must see the king" (Esther 4:16)*. What courage, what determination displayed by a young woman who got it all, and in a moment was willing to lose it for the sake of saving a people who had a promise. What also stands out about this story is the beauty pageant held for King Ahasuerus to replace the Queen, and the role played by a little Jewish girl who was not from the land of the king but was part of God's divine providence.

The writer tells us that there were many beautiful women from every province of his kingdom. But the difference between Esther and the other beautiful women was that she is chosen; she was called to help deliver God's people from their extinction by the wicked Haman. She was from the seed of Abraham. God would not assign her to be a "concubine," a secondary position. For when God chooses to use you, even if you were a concubine before God chose you, **He** starts a work **in** you that He is well able to perform. His work will elevate you to the stature of "Queen," first received in your spirit and then actualized in your body.

You may not believe it can happen to you but look at Rahab. God used her because she wanted to be used by God. She was willing to sacrifice her own life by hiding the spies in her Inn. Had they been caught, she along with the men would have been killed. But God, who looks on the heart, not only forgave her, but also put her in line for the greatest blessing of her life. She met one of the princes of the Israelites, named Salmon, married and had children. One of them was a son named Boaz, who was the father of Obed by Ruth, and Obed was the father of Jesse. Jesse was the father of David the king through whom came our king of kings and Lord of lords, Jesus the Christ, the Son of God.

The Messiah's family came through Rahab, whose life was changed. She desired to know the God of the Israelites and her desire was fulfilled. God did not forget, and He did not feel she was unworthy to be in the bloodline or family lineage, because her past life was full of scandal and immorality. When God accepts you in the beloved, you are changed and cleansed and your sins are remitted; making you justified, just as if you never sinned. Hallelujah! If you please God, make Him the center of your attention and affection, obey His commandments or life principles and you will be blessed. If He did it for Rahab, he can do it for you! God will sanctify you for His use. He didn't and never would have put her in sin to accomplish His purpose. He doesn't take a person down from where He meets them. He meets them where they are and begins to lift them up. Praise God! You are about to be taken up.

The book of Esther tells us how Mordecai had raised his younger cousin Esther (Hadassah) because both of her parents were dead. Mordecai was divinely directed to take care of her because God had a plan for his people. She was to have a part in bringing it to pass. A young girl with no guardian who could be trusted was an open target for all sorts of tragedy and wickedness by men. Mordecai was concerned, not only for Esther's present circumstances, but also for her future. I'm sure he thought about this responsibility that if anything happened to him, who would care for Esther? So hearing about the king's state and what he was about to do, he approached his young precious cousin, Esther. He told her to enter the beauty pageant for the King's new wife.

We are told that Esther was "beautiful of form", (her figure and face). She was included to be among women placed in the custody of Hegai, the eunuch in charge of the king's harem. Although she was obedient to Mordecai, I don't believe that she wanted to go. The scriptures say she "was taken." In the Hebrew positive, this suggests that she was taken by force. After all, she didn't pick this assignment; it was selected for her. Yet she did not complain.

Sometimes we are dealt things we don't expect from life day after day. Jesus said that in the world, ye should have tribulation, but be of good cheer *(John 16:33)*, or take courage; I have overcome the world. One would ask, what do you mean Jesus? I'm hurting right now! My children are taking me through, my job is taking me through, be of good cheer? Yes, because I have overcome the world, and I can tell you what to do. All you have to do is listen to Jesus and rely on the Holy Spirit to lead you according to God's Word. Then, just obey. The Word of God tells me in *(Romans 8:28/NASB), "And we know that God causes all things to work together for good to those who love God, to those who are called according to His purpose."* The end result will be good.

Esther was being groomed to be one of the kings' concubines. She was prepared to go before the king with the other contenders. She would take all of the finery and jewels that were available to her to win the king's approval and desire. It might seem as though she really didn't care what the king thought. Perhaps she really didn't want to win. Or maybe she knew that if she won though she was beautiful among the other beautiful virgins in the land that it would take more than the external, more than a few trinkets, or a new hairstyle, manicure, or pedicure. All of these things are good but if all of them had these attributes, what would be the difference? One woman was just as beautiful as the other. She would need an edge or an advantage over the others.

Esther was a daughter, a Jew, different from the Persian women and many of the other women from various cultures. God had a plan for Esther, despite the loss of her parents, despite this seemingly desperate position she faced. Esther won the favor of the king's head eunuch over his harem. Hegai took Esther and separated her from the other women in the harem and moved her to the king's palace. Esther pleased the eunuch Hegai and found favor with him. He gave her the best the palace had to offer, providing choice maids, cosmetics, and food fit for a Queen. He transferred her and her maids to the best section of the palace. Before she became a Queen, she was being prepared on how to conduct herself as a Queen. She literally lived like a Queen. This was all in the direction of the next level in her future.

Often, before you go to the next level, you will be shifted and get into unfamiliar territory, not particularly sure why you are where you are. But it is all part of the plan set in motion. The Holy Spirit is taking you into new areas. Favor is being poured out on you. After all you have been through, you may be wondering what is happening now. Just as Hegai was being used to bring Esther into her destiny, so God through the Holy Spirit and the events in your life is bringing you into your destiny. You do have a purpose despite your past or present state of affairs. Esther only wanted what Hegai wanted for her and instructed her to take when it was time to go before the king.

We need to get to the place that we say, Lord; all I want is what you want for me. Show me how to conduct myself, teach me how to dress like your lady. Teach me how to talk like your lady. Teach me how to win your affection and favor. God will reveal to you secrets that will shower you with His divine favor because He knows He has your heart. Good God that He is!

So, Esther listened to Hegai's instructions as she went before the king. I don't know what number she was, whether she was first or last. It did not matter how many other women were before her or after her, when you have the favor of God. Esther went in to the king in the 10th month of Tebeth, in the 7th year of his reign. The scriptures say the king loved Esther more than all the other women and she found favor and kindness with him more than all the other virgins. He set the royal crown on her head and made her Queen instead of Vashti.

Who you believe is your competition may not be. You will never have to compete for a mate. You don't have to compete for what God gives you. No matter how beautiful you are, there is someone as beautiful or more beautiful than you. There are many men who are not necessarily looking for the most beautiful girl in the world. Yes, every man wants an attractive woman. You can be attractive at any size, any shade, and shape. But he also wants a woman who can handle life's situations with him, and encourage him as he works to provide and cover his household. A saved mate is more importantly interested in your spiritual state first. Just as God set up Esther, likewise he is setting you up to be blessed.

The providence of God is seen throughout this book. We begin to see the hand of God moving. The move of God or the setting up of events according to His foreknowledge is His divine "providence"-from the Latin words "pro" and "video" carrying the meaning "to see beforehand and provide what is needed." Provide comes from those same two words, the Hebrew translated "provide" is ra'ah' and means "to see," the same idea. The providence of God is clearly seen in the lives of Mordecai, Esther, and the Jews of Persia.

- Esther's parents died, and Mordecai took care of her, raising her as his own daughter.

- Mordecai had a position at the king's gate and heard about the search for a Queen.

- Esther won the favor of the chief eunuch, Hegai.

- Hegai separated her from the other contenders and took her to the palace.

- When it was time for Esther to go before the king, Hegai advised her and she does as he said.

  - The king chose Esther and loved her more than all the other women in his harem.

  - The King made Esther Queen over Vashti.

- After Esther became Queen, Mordecai discovered a plot against King Ahasureus and told Esther who told the king and saved his life.

- The King's insomnia that brought to light Mordecai's deed of kindness.

- The King's apparent memory loss that lead him to favor one of the Jews he had agreed to have killed.

- The King's deep concern for Esther's welfare, when he had a harem to choose from.

God is sovereign and knows all things.

Job 2:2 "I know that thou canst do all things and that no purpose of thine can be thwarted." (NASB)

Proverbs 21:1 "The King's heart is like channels of water in the hand of the Lord, He turns it wherever He wishes." (NASB)

More than anything else, we should desire the favor of God. Seek Him, for though we run after the favor of men, this will not get you to the palace. This will not crown you Queen. When God's favor is with you, your king will see you in a light different and apart from all other women. God will not let you blend in with all the others. We heavily concentrate on the outward adornment, and I believe we should look our best. But this is a time when we all begin to look like carbon copies of each other. Some new hair, new nail designs, the latest make-up. Clones of today's what's hot and what's not! We can lack what we need inwardly, which can be realized by all those who look upon us. That is our relationship with the Lord, our love for Him causes us to stand up and stand out. It is what gives us that edge over all the others, though they may have the figure we desire, or the hair, or the complexion. Remember, your king's heart is in His hands.

Don't Play with A Player

Recently, I read an article in a very popular women's magazine dealing with the confessions of a "player." For those of you not familiar with this term, it identifies a man or woman who takes pleasure in having simultaneous multiple relationships and satisfying each one while enlarging their ego for their skill. The old term was "Don Juan," or playboy or playgirl. The article had Q&A responses between the male subject and the interviewer. He was asked about the number of women he was sleeping with. He answered that there were currently four, beside his number "one" girlfriend, -a total of five.

Now consider that these five women may be spending intimate time with other partners in between visits from this player. I'm sure that despite his huge ego, if the truth be told, he is not truly satisfying all of them sexually. In all likelihood, he is providing companionship, something some women need while tolerating the lack of sexual gratification. I wonder if the women he is attending to have ever thought about the expanding number of those who may be riding on this merry go round of sexual partners.

In essence, this man is doing what was done back in the biblical times, securing a concubine to meet his needs. He could have whatever he wanted whenever he wanted, because it was the concubine's task to make him happy, to bring him pleasure. He did not necessarily have the confining laws of marriage with a concubine. The concubine of those times understood that. The problem today is that the women don't understand that they are living the life of the concubine when they enter into a relationship where there is sexual intercourse before and without marriage. When you enter into this type of relationship, you must understand what this means for you and for him.

The women being used by this player may feel safe because they have taken some means of protection by use of condoms.

That's scary, considering that condoms can't protect you from some STD's. Your relationship with the Lord will also be diminished. Condemnation and separation in your heart from Him comes with every moment of weakness, until you are cold and empty. The problem is that sin deceives you in the beginning. Then when you are caught in the trap, there are painful consequences. Some women still get pregnant during sexual intercourse while using a condom. How? Condoms do have microscopic tears and holes, but they are defenseless against skin-to-skin contact!!

In the article, this player was proud to say he treated his concubines better than other men with whom they had been. Unfortunately, they are so discouraged by settling for a life as a concubine; providing another man physical pleasure without a commitment for occasional nights of bliss, which will eventually become tiring. It will leave you wanting more and receiving very little in return. When asked about his hierarchical order of treatment of these women, he pointed out that his girlfriend is on the top of his pyramid (she's official and is taken to all public events and special gatherings). There is a number two woman, but the others fall in order of need and time. **He** was aware of the needs of each (sex-attention-etc.) and believed he was more than satisfactorily satisfying them. The number two woman gets some expensive trinkets because she's settling for secrecy. **He** compensates her, because she knows there is a number one woman in his life. She is hoping that eventually she may have a shot at replacing number one, should things not work out. However, he shared with the interviewer that this number two woman is not number one material. To him, number one material is someone who has no history or a very small history with other men.

How long can anyone who steps into his trap avoid a history with other men, when many do as he does? Love them and leave them for another. The woman goes on to try and find someone who will truly be her number one partner for life. And after she's shared everything, she has with him, he decides to move on-with someone else.

So naturally, she is building a history.

My sisters, beware! This is not what our Lord would have you settle for. This vulnerable woman has settled for someone who will never see her as a wife or number one girlfriend. She is just a fill-in, like a stunt double. When the original cast member has a hard scene to do and refuses to or feels it is too risky for them, a double is called. The double doesn't get much credit publicly, but the scene looks good. We, as women of God, daughters of the King were never meant to be stunt doubles-secondary wives, concubines.

But for many sisters, this has become the sad reality. A few trinkets have covered up the fact that he values what he receives from you and wants to keep you around for a while. But he doesn't want to make a commitment. You must take responsibility to safeguard your heart and your spirit from the tactics of the enemy. You accomplish that by relying on God's Word and living a holy separated life. You deserve more, and your Heavenly Father designed you for better. This is not a man who has made a vow to God and intends to keep it. This is not a man who esteems godly women, and what one has to offer. This is a foolish man who knows not the scripture. But you should know them and obey them.

1 Corinthians 7:1-2 -" Now concerning the things about which you wrote, it is good for a man not to touch a woman. But because of immoralities, each man is to have his own wife, and each woman is to have her own husband." (NASR)

In *I Corinthians 6:20* we are told, *"glorify God in your body."* When we do God's will in obedience, we win. When we refuse to obey, we lose. The world is always competing with Christians for their love, the love of this world and the things of this world take away and diminish the love we have for God. There are things we must do.

> *1 Thessalonians 4:3-4 "It is God's will that you should be sanctified: that you should avoid sexual immorality; that each of you learn to control his own body in a way that is holy and honorable." (NIV)*

The number "two" woman wanted more, but didn't think she could have it with anyone else. She did what she did knowing about his girlfriend, knowing that he was sharing himself between their beds. He further points out that if and when he broke up with his number one girl-with whom he shared everything except honesty he would more than likely wind up with someone he was flirting with and maintained a platonic relationship, rather than a sex partner. This is the best that an unregenerate heart has to offer. One woman will never be enough for him, and the best thing that the number two woman could have happen is that they break up. *"The heart is more deceitful than all else and is desperately sick; who can understand it? I, the Lord, search the heart, I test the mind, Even to give to each man according to his ways, According to the results of his deeds" (Jeremiah 17:910/NASB).* The player's lifestyle will eventually catch up to him, in one way or another.

This player then gives advice to those who really want to become number one to any man.

- Hold out on the sex.

- Flirt with him and hold his hand.

- Kiss him and let him get an idea of how good the sex might be. BUT DO NOT SLEEP WITH **HIM!!!**

I agree with the first and the last tips. He declared that men always want what they can't have. He concludes that he doesn't feel guilty at all about what he does. He has been so blinded by the enemy that he doesn't know whatever you do unto God's children, you have done it as unto Him. The Lord takes the tears of his children and particularly his daughter's personally *(Mathew 18:10)*.

But daughters know that He has put a plan in place for you to follow to avoid being destroyed by the enemy's tactics. Don't play around with a player, whether he is in the church or out of the church. Remember, "your body is the temple of the Holy Spirit who is in you, whom you have from God, and that you are not your own" *(1 Corinthians 6:19)*. The writer of Hebrews said:

> *"Marriage should be honored by all, and the marriage bed kept pure, for God will judge the adulterer and all the sexually immoral."* (Hebrew 13:4NASB)

The scriptures teach that sex is for marriage and that it is to be a monogamous relationship, all "players" need not apply!!

Wait, Wait, Wait, Again I Say Wait!

> *"But they that wait upon the Lord shall renew their strength; they shall mount up with wings as eagles; they shall run, and not be weary; and they shall walk, and not faint." (Isaiah 40:31/Dickson NASE)*

Here is a promise to those who are willing to wait for God to move at his appointed time. Often instead of waiting for God to move, we try to move God to act at our desired time. It is no wonder how we can be influenced with **all** of the T.V. commercials selling everything from toothpaste to cereal and milk with sexual messages. All of the advice we receive on television from leading experts has not cured a man's desire for something beautiful and pure. And society is trying to achieve this desire by lesser means. They are settling for "nutra-sex" -artificial substitutes for pure holy fulfilled sex (spiritually and naturally), which **in** the long run cause cancer in a relationship naturally and spiritually.

Ephesians 5:3 admonishes those who profess Christ within the church in regard to sexual sins, *"let it not be once named among you, as becometh saints."* Despite what the media projects, everybody is not "doing it." The enemy (Satan) is so subtle. He will whisper **in** your ear and tell you, "go ahead just a little squeeze and a kiss, you're strong enough. You don't have to go all the way, don't be scared, nothing will happen." And before you know it, you have squeezed and kissed your way into something you didn't mean to have happen.

I just believe, from personal experience, that if you wait on the Lord, He will make it worth the wait! If many women would be honest, they would admit that sex is an empty pleasure without the love, trust, and commitment of a man who loves you, and you alone. You would feel completely safe in his arms when you can trust him with your heart. The reason you could ever trust any man would be, because he honors God in a covenant relationship with himself, you, and God. Also, he would not violate God's laws or His holiness. You must understand that a covenant relationship binds the two partners into an irrevocable agreement with God. It has deeper meaning than just going to say, "I Do", and if it doesn't work out, you can both get a divorce. No, a covenant agreement says, "I'll stay no matter how hard it gets, I'll believe God and pray through our tests and trials. I'll let the Word of God be my final word and authority. If a man can't offer to do this and follow through, he's not a King or a King's kid and therefore you can't be his Queen.

If he is not willing to make a promise to God, from former evidence that God will do all to stand by those he makes "wait," then he is not ready to be your covenant partner.

The scriptures tell us, *"Be careful for nothing (in nothing be anxious); but in every thing by prayer and supplication with thanksgiving let your requests be made known unto God. And the peace of God, which passeth all understanding, shall keep (guard) your hearts and minds (thoughts) through Christ Jesus"* (Philippians 4:6-7/Dickson NASB)).

Regardless of what you've done in the past, the scriptures tell us to cast off our former way of life. In other words, get rid of it. Stop it, now! Jesus said, the day you hear my voice harden not your heart. The Lord speaks to you in His word, in prayer, in your spirit and he even uses literature you read and conversations with others. While speaking of others, let me say here, when people speak into your life and say, "the Lord said", make sure what they say does not contradict what the "Word" says. This is vital if you are going to allow it to have any validity in your decision-making. The Holy Spirit has been sent to lead you and guide you into "all truth" and "all righteousness."

Another deception the devil will create is if you're not having sexual intercourse or vaginal penetration, then you are still pure despite the fact that you are doing other things to gratify you sexually in order to produce an orgasm.

In scripture we are told, *"For this is the will of God, even your sanctification, that ye should abstain from fornication: That every one of you should Know how to possess his vessel in sanctification and honor; not in the lust of concupiscence, even as the Gentiles, which know not God."* (1 Thessalonians 4:3-5/Dickson NASB)

You don't want to trigger any desires to go all the way by any gestures you make. You don't want to arouse any male to the point he would conclude you want to go all the way. Most times, it can be the most innocent gestures, which can escalate to heavy passion, depending on the person's sensitivity to touch. For some, holding hands is okay. For others, it may be too much stimulation. So, you want to be careful to close the gate to any progressive sexual immorality.

The time will come when you will be able to enjoy all the pleasures of marriage that God has ordained, but you must be patient. *Hebrew 10:36 says:*

"For ye have need of patience, that after ye have done the will of God, ye might receive the promise" (Dickson NASB)

You can't lose if you do the will of God. He will honor those who do His will. Stand on the Word of God and never mind the voice and taunting of the devil, for he knows your blessing will come. At the end of God's will is the believer's blessing!

The spiritual reasoning should be enough, but if not, allow me to give you some medical motivation. Consider some of the physical consequences. Despite the media perpetuation of safe sex with the use of condoms, the truth is they provide little protection against sexually transmitted diseases. The Human Papilloma Virus (HPV) is the most common virus STD causing more than 2.5 million new infections each year. HPV is incurable, uncomfortable and gross. It causes genital warts; but even more importantly, it causes more than 90% of all cervical cancers. A condom provides no protection against **HPV**. It is just not safe against it at all! Protect your body, which is the temple of the Holy Spirit and abstain until you are in covenant with a partner who will protect his body and yours.

Waiting

Here I sit and wait for my mate

No longer a worldly woman

Setting traps, being bait

I am now a child of the King

With the hope of eternal life

On Earth my Father promised to

Withhold no good thing

Thus, I wait for my true love's arrival

The Spirit of God, the source of my survival.

By Sonya L. Caldwell

Journal Page

(What Thoughts Did The Holy Spirit Give You In This Chapter?)

"Do not be yoked together with unbelievers. For what do righteousness and wickedness have in common? Or what fellowship can light have with darkness."
(2 Corinthians 6:14)

CHAPTER FIVE

Some Things You Need To Know

Some Things You Need To Know

In this day when we are trying to get believers to know their rights in Christ and to receive all that the Lord has for them; the message of holiness is being somewhat downplayed--though not intentionally. But as spiritual leaders we are to raise our voices like a trumpet and show people, including saints the error of their ways, in love and provide restoration and reconciliation.

> *Hosea 4: 6-9 "My people are destroyed for lack of knowledge: because thou hast rejected knowledge, I will also reject thee, that thou shalt be no priest to me: seeing thou hast forgotten the law of thy God, I will also forget thy children. As they were increased, so they sinned against me: therefore will I change their glory into shame. They eat up the sin of my people, and they set their heart on their iniquity. And there shall be, like people, like priest: and I will punish them for their ways, and reward them their Doings" (Dickson NASB).*

In that time, the people brought an offering to the priests each time they sinned, and the priests received a portion of the offering. The more the people sinned, the more the people blessed the priests, until the priests received so much that they shared it with other relatives. At other times, they resold what they received and made profits from the people's sins. The profit from the people's sins gave them power and position in the community.

So instead of leading the people out of sin, they encouraged sin to increase their profits. No true woman of God wants to be guilty of profiting from the people's sin because they have gained popularity and notoriety in the community by not preaching and teaching against sin. Our voices must be a clarion reminder of what God expects of us as his children and daughters.

This book reflects my attempt to tell you some things you need to know, how to live a life that is pleasing to the Lord, and one that will save you from spiritual and natural death. Closely read this chapter and journal your thoughts at the end so you can see the progression of your spiritual insight and thoughts. I believe the Lord will communicate by His Spirit for you and from you.

What You Don't Know Can Hurt You!

"Wise men lay-up knowledge: but the mouth of the foolish is near destruction." (Proverbs 10:14/ Dickson NASB)

" My people are destroyed for lack of knowledge: because thou hast rejected knowledge, I will also reject thee seeing thou hast forgotten the law of thy God, I will also forget thy children." (Hosea 4:6/Dickson NASB)

There are some students who because the class time is long, fall asleep. At the time they do so, the most important information is given. There is information throughout this book. Please don't brush over it. It can save your relationship and your spiritual and natural life! Facts are sometimes boring. But you must see the hard truth and know the consequences for wrong actions and responses. This is a day when we must lift up our voices as trumpets in Zion and show God's people where they are in error. It is so easy to fall into error when you want to do right.

You have the world, the flesh, and the devil to fight against, but know "greater is He that is in you than he that is in the world."

In trying to develop a potential lasting relationship leading to a covenant agreement, getting into the physical aspect of sex before emotional aspects of trust, security, and mutual respect are developed can cripple a possibly lasting loving relationship, according to Josh McDowell. He also cites in his book *(Why True Love Waits)* that there are studies, which show that 50 percent of the people who get married have been engaged at least once before. So it is not safe to say, since we're engaged it's all right to go ahead and have sex because we'll be married soon anyway.

God has set boundaries and we should obey them. They are for our own protection and well-being. What seems to be confining is really divine protection against physical, psychological, emotional, and spiritual damage; which could last for a lifetime without Christ.

There is more to the act of sex than just physical gratification. Becoming "one flesh" happens **in** the spirit person of the individual as well as in the physical. It is a mystical union, which is why so many minds are messed up now. They have become one with too many spirits, leaving an imprint on their own spirit. Beside this there are medical consequences which should be seriously considered and are noted by Josh McDowell in his book *"Why True Love Waits/Tyndale House Publishers/Copyright 2002)*

- Today more Americans are infected with sexually transmitted diseases (STDs) than at any other time in history. (pg. 36-37)

- There are as many as 45 million cases in just the U.S. of genital herpes. (pg. 37)

- The latest estimates indicate that there are 15 million new STD cases each year in the U.S., about half of which contract lifelong infections that are incurable. (pg. 38)

- An estimated 56 million Americans have an incurable viral STD other than **HIV,** such as genital herpes or human papillomavirus (HPV). That is more than one in five Americans.

- Dr. W. Cates estimates that a staggering 65 million Americans have an incurable STD. (pg. 37)

- Worldwide, an estimated 333 million new cases of four curable STDs (gonorrhea, chlamydia infection, syphilis, and trichomoniasis) occurred among adults 15 to 49 years of age in 1995. (pg. 37)

- An estimated one million Americans are infected with human immunodeficiency virus **(HIV).**

- An estimated 5.5 million new infections occur each year with at least 20 million people currently infected. (pg. 233)

- There is no single STD epidemic, but rather multiple epidemics. (pg. 233)

- As many as 45 million Americans may already be infected with HPV at some point in their lives. (pg. 233)

- Between 5 and 5.5 million individuals are newly infected with **HPV** each year. (pg. 233)

- Between 50 and 75 percent of sexually active individuals are now, or have previously been, infected with **HPV.** (pg. 233)

- Only 2 percent of men or women have symptoms of infection. (pg. 233)

- **[HPV]** is the cause of more than 90 percent of all cervical cancer. (pg. 233)

- A 1998 report of sexually active women at Rutgers University showed that 60 percent tested positive for human papillomavirus (HPV) at some time during the three-year study. (pg. 233)

- **HPV** causes nearly all cases of cervical cancer. Cervical cancer annually causes the death of approximately 5,000 American women and 250,000 women worldwide. (pg. 233)

- Because of their patterns transmissibility, genital herpes, syphilis, and **HPV** can all be transmitted by mutual masturbation. In fact, a recent study demonstrates that many individuals with genital warts transmit the HPV virus on their fingertips. (pg. 233)

Don't be deceived as Eve was, "I was deceived and I ate." The battle began then and continues to this day. But there is victory in light of God's word, for understanding this and receiving this knowledge will enable the believer to build a relationship and continue after marriage than to allow ignorance to tear it down!

It's Not Too Late To Say No!

"for he is a liar, and the father of it." (John 8:44/ Dickson NASE)

Connecting the Pharisees to the devil in their deeds, Jesus said of the devil that he is a liar. So the Pharisees were acting like their father for they had the same spirit. The devil is a deceiver, a liar and he constructs each lie according to the needs and desires of his victims. But if we would obey God's word and do all that He commands us to do, it would be for our good that he might preserve us alive *(Deuteronomy 6:24)*

One of the lines the devil uses to keep a woman operating after the lust of her flesh or after her emotional needs is "don't stop now, you're no longer a virgin so it doesn't really matter." He'll make you feel as though you have nothing left to give because you're only going to give the new intended what you gave all the other pretenders. But not so! You can give him your new innocence. Abstaining gives you back a spiritual purity and integrity; and recaptures your self-esteem and valuable worth before the Lord. You will find a new respect for you and your body. Your fellowship with the Lord will be strengthened because of your obedience to God. Obedience is better than sacrifice.

It is possible to say no, because the Bible says that our heavenly Father "hath delivered us from the power of darkness and hath translated us into the kingdom of his Son" (Colossians 1:13). Satan has no power over you any longer. You have the power to say "no" to any sexual immorality. What was done before is under the blood and you are taking a stand for Christ.

You have been translated from the Kingdom of Satan to the Kingdom of Jesus Christ. Christ's kingdom is governed by opposite standards than Satan's. The word of God says, *"marriage is honorable in all and the bed is undefiled" (Hebrew 13:4)*. If a man truly loves you, not just your shape, your face, your hair, or any superficial reason, but loves your "Spirit" he will wait if he has intentions of marriage. **He** won't pressure you either. It would surely take a man with a heart of God to see the value of being celibate until marriage. Even if you become engaged, still wait for the covenant ceremony, when he will crown you his ***"Queen."***

You must remember to never let any man throw it up in your face that, "you have had sex with all your other boyfriends, so why not me?" Once you make up your mind to live a sexually pure life, only to be shared with your covenant partner, the devil will pull out all the stops. **He** sends back old boyfriends you haven't heard from in a long time, some with whom you've shared memorable intimacies. He'll give you flashbacks to arouse all those old feelings, never showing the consequences of giving **in** to them. The response to, "why not me" could be "because I honor God now." I respect myself and my body more now as the temple of God. God is so in me that I will not take him into the bed of fornication with us. I respect my husband whoever he will be "now." The scriptures teach us, as the light appears walk therein. Or as you receive understanding, walk in it.

If he can't understand this no matter what he professes as his faith in Christ, he does not love Jesus nor respect His word as the ultimate authority. I safely say this because Jesus said, *"if you love me keep my commandments." (John 14:15)*

Aside from this the Bible says that no fornicator shall inherit the kingdom of God *(1 Corinthians 6:9)*. The Corinthians were heavily into sexual immorality, because it was a part of their worship, but Paul says, *"... such were some of you, but ye are washed, but ye are justified in the Name of the Lord, and by the Spirit of our God."* No man, I repeat, No man is worth losing favor with God and no man *is worth the condemnation you will feel if you disobey God. The Lord will forgive you if you repent, but you will feel so let down and the devil will try to rob you of your self-esteem. The devil's aim is to make you feel bad about you. It's all a mind game to him, that is why you must use the mighty weapons of God against every high thing that exalteth itself against the knowledge of God, and bringing into captivity every thought to the obedience of Christ (2 Corinthians 10:5)*

Your eyes become opened after you sin, just as Eve's were opened after Adam joined her in the sin. The devil will never show you the wrong doing of your sins before you commit them. He's clever enough not to let you feel it until it's too late to reverse the order. Let's think about it, if he did you would not go that far. While there is restoration and forgiveness there is also pain, disappointment, regret and deeper sorrow than you could have imagined. Yet, on the other hand, it is so uplifting and glorious to have the victory of doing it God's way! It is a spiritual high to have the victory over temptation. Recognize that you are more valuable than your material possessions. I say this because some women will give their bodies to a man faster than they would give him their car or keys to their house. Well, if you can't trust him with these things, how can you trust him with your most precious gift, you and your body? Women are receivers and men are transferees or givers. When you become one with him, you receive from his spirit as well as from his physical being. Are you sure you know all that is locked into his "spirit?" Even if you think you do, you don't. But you can in time find out much more. If a man won't respect your care or any thing you would entrust to him, a little hint, he's not ready for a sacred act performed in a covenant relationship. Men will only value what you value highly.

If Jesus purchased your redemption, which cost nothing less than his own blood, isn't this a clue to how much you are worth to him! Oh, please wait.

No More Toys or Gadgets

There doesn't seem to be any dignified way to talk on the subject of *"sexual self-gratification,"* so I'll cut straight to the chase. The enemy has conjured up lies about the acceptance and justification for doing this, and society has bought into this deception; even some silently who profess Christianity. Some believe that if there has been no vaginal penetration, they are still pure. Let me say here while Satan has created perversions of sex, sex itself is not dirty. God designed it for two partners of the opposite sex to enjoy. Sex is not some dirty little secret, or a necessary duty, but a beautiful act created by God with deep spiritual meaning. The sacred act of sexual intercourse is so sacred that any form of manipulation by magazines, gadgets, toys, or pornography to help oneself arrive at an orgasm in the absence of a partner is masturbation and unholy. God said, *"be ye holy, for I am holy" (1 Peter 1:16).*

This gift is designed and reserved for married covenant partners. Who is your partner if you are stimulating yourself to get physical gratification? What spirit are you in covenant with? Which master have you obeyed and become a servant of? When doing these things, you have reduced the most beautiful act to just another act of fun or pleasure which you alone control. Not with love, for there is no one to physically love you or become one with you. But you have joined yourself to Satan's perversions, which could affect you eventually physically and emotionally. I have read of people being so affected by this that it could take years to get natural feelings of satisfaction back to normal for some married couples.

Some people, even those who are married, have fallen into an addiction for some devices, they say because of boredom. Which is another lie the devil created, for he knows the "law of diminishing return" (Tim Alan Gardner/ Sacred Sex WaterBrook Press/ Copyright 2002), which states that when the single focus of any activity is getting pleasure and physical gratification (or fun), then the level of pleasure one gains from that activity will diminish with time. Then, in order to receive the same level of gratification that was previously enjoyed, one would have to increase the pleasure stimuli. Always looking for more or a way to a greater high than the last one, because the old high can't satisfy you.

There is a physical progression to want more than the last. Holding hands was all right on the first date, but next time you'll want to put your arms around each other and kiss because that was not enough. Before you know it, if you haven't set safe boundaries not to cross, you will get weaker and weaker if you don't seal the boundaries with prayer and the Word of God.

God has designed this act of intimacy to represent the intimacy between our Savior, the Groom and us, His Bride The Church *(Ephesians 5:31-32)*. This is the mystical union that Paul shared with the Church. This act is never to be reduced to simple "lust." These kinds of things will only further stimulate you to engage in sex with someone who isn't even thinking of making a commitment to you and make you vulnerable for a far lesser relationship. Don't even start! Get rid of the idea immediately when Satan plants it.

I once overheard some co-workers speaking of a lingerie party one of the girls had given. From the way they were talking, that party sounded like a promotion for pornography. The wrong spirit was in attendance. They were not there to buy beautiful nightwear, but to promote sexual promiscuity with the use of such gadgets and toys! This is just another opportunity for the devil to bind many souls in sexual immorality.

But obey the word to put away the filth of the flesh, which makes a mockery out of God's holy and sacred plan of pleasure for His married couples. The Bible teaches us that as we come into truth, we are to walk in the light as he is in the light. If this has been a part of your former lifestyle, cast it off and embrace the Love of Christ for you and his cleansing forgiveness. Throw out any items of bondage. Let the Lord renew your mind and cleanse your spirit so there will be no repeats.

A Lesson From Two Women

The story of Sarah and Hagar teaches us about the cost of being anxious about what we want and the cost of not waiting on God to do what He said He would do, **in His** time.

Sarah couldn't wait on God to give her a baby as promised. So being confused and impatient, she thought that a law outside of God's commandment, because it was part of society's norm, would be all right. She did not realize that the Holy God would never compromise His holiness to give those he loves a blessing. His blessings are holy and they will be delivered through a holy route.

Hagar perhaps thought she would gain much, not realizing the emotional consequences. She only looked at what good could happen, if it turned out all right. She didn't weigh the consequences; she didn't consider, what if my mistress doesn't like me, or what if I am unable to let go of my child and his father?

Sexual intimacy is totally a spiritual experience, meaning that something deeper happens than just a climatic conclusion and a euphoric feeling. Seconds, or maybe minutes after it's over, the true feelings for each other come clear. You either love the person or just enjoyed the moment.

After Abraham finished with Hagar, he still loved Sarah. He was attached to his son and not necessarily Hagar. In *(Genesis 21:11)* it states that when Sarah wanted Abraham to put out Hagar and her son, "it was very grievous in Abraham's sight because of his son." It would seem as though he had no attachments emotionally to Hager, though she opened up the fountain of her life, to bear a son for him. Perhaps, she hoped it would change their relationship. Hopefully, it would make her equal with Sarah, his wife, to whom he was committed.

If so, her plans failed. A man she tried to please could not stand up for her. She is cast out with no hope for her child, or family to whom to return. She separated herself from her child. Oh, the heavy disappointment of the way her life had turned out. The child had not brought hoped for promises. The scriptures said she cast him under one of the shrubs and separated herself. She couldn't bear to watch the child die slowly.

Hagar began to weep and lift up her voice. I don't know whether she called on the God of Abraham or on the God of her lands. But Abraham's God responded to the cry of the lad, for *Genesis 21:17* said, *"And God heard the voice of the lad; and the angel of God called to Hagar out of heaven.... for God hath heard the voice of the lad where he is"* (Dickson NASB).

This hopeless, helpless, betrayed young woman, a single mother who saw no way out of her dilemma, had God do something marvelous for her. He did not want her or her child to die like this. Her death would have been the result of hopelessness and blindness. But the one who is our only help and hope, which can open the eyes of the blind, showed Hagar hope and gave her life when she had settled for death. It says in verse 19, *"And God opened her eyes"*, *He showed her a well, their source for survival and also a promise to make her son great!*

Oh, if only we would let God open our eyes and show us a better way. He has come that we might have life and have it more abundantly! God opened Hagar's eyes and showed her a well of water, and she went. After revealing the life source, she made a decision to go for life. Regardless of the pain and hurt, God has lifegiving water to cause you to live emotionally and physically and be the mother or woman you need to be, despite your past experiences. If you are ready to give up and say there's no hope, I'll never get someone to love me and place me first after God, I want to lead you to Jesus who said he would put in us a well of waterspringing up into everlasting life *(John 4:14)*.

I direct your attention to Jesus, the only fountain of living water. After drinking from this fountain, you will never thirst again. Understand that I am directing your attention, your focus, your desire to Jesus not the church, not the people, not the pastor, but only to Jesus. The pastor is your earthly shepherd who leads others as God leads him. But Jesus has promised to never leave you or forsake you!

Let's Pray! Heavenly Father,

I desire to be the daughter you can hold up as a light to help others follow me as I follow you. Help me to show forth strength to walk as a woman of integrity and virtue and resist the devil and his temptations to be disobedient, weak and helpless to his seductions. Right now, I declare to be strong in the Lord and the power of your might. You have endowed me with power. I will, by the power invested in me and the blood of Jesus Christ, stand against the wiles of the devil and put him in flight! I will encourage and strengthen my sisters in Christ to walk worthy of the vocation wherewith we are called as saints to live holy and righteously in this present world. I will bring you glory and honor, by glorifying you in my body!!

Love,

Your Daughter

Journal Page

(What Thoughts Did The Holy Spirit Give You In This Chapter?)

"For I know the plans I have for you," declares the Lord, *"plans to prosper you and not to harm you, plans to give you hope* and a future." (Jeremiah 29:11)

CHAPTER SIX

The Bite of The Vampire

The Bite of The Vampire

When the vampire bit his victim, it insured that his needs would be met. He would have a woman who would supply his needs and exist in the same fashion as him. He made his victim like himself, and he used victims for his own purposes. The women were always seductively dressed and seeking blood in a lustful fashion. He seduced them and sucked their blood.

Isn't that just like the devil? He brings out the need for some men to insup;;/ re a partner like themselves (and some women do the same). Only when he bites them and transfers what is in him to them, can he be sure to secure his future partnership. He must make them become as he is. So he seduces them until he can get close enough to make them vulnerable and too weak to resist. At their weakest moment, he takes the Bite!

The devil is like the vampire working in the darkness of our lives, looking for an opportune moment to strike. That is why we must draw very near to JESUS especially at the low points of our lives. When you feel yourself growing weak, and we know when that is, we must run to Him and ask Him to strengthen us. The apostle Paul writes in *I Corinthians 10:13 (Dickson NASB) about temptation, "...but God is faithful, who will not suffer you to be tempted above that ye are able; but will with the temptation also make a way to escape, that ye may be able to bear it."*

I would like to share a story with you about a young woman who will be anonymous and a young man she dated, who will also remain anonymous. Sarah was a sweet young woman who loved the Lord. She demonstrated her love through charitable acts of kindness to those in need and her faithfulness to her local church services by duties performed when asked. She was active in her home church and always very busy, but she was still lonely at times. She worked full-time and began taking classes at night to fill her empty hours of loneliness. She had been delivered from many issues in her past, which the devil had used to hold her hostage. At the very time she felt strong in the Lord, the enemy came knocking on her door. He usually tries to appear as an angel of light, and this time would be no different.

While registering for her next class, she met a young man named Todd. Her first impression was that he seemed very nice as he signed up for a class at the same time. They began to talk while they were waiting in line to register. Soon, they discovered that they would have one class together. Todd felt he would have a hard time with that subject. It was one of Sarah's easier areas of study and he asked if she would tutor him or help him if the work became too stressful.

Sarah was more than happy to help since helping was part of her nature. In a way, she needed to be needed. What Sarah didn't know was that Todd used registration to meet and then prey on new victims. He would sign up and before the deadline for reimbursement, he would drop out of the class. By then, he would have met and gotten all the information about his next victim.

Sarah did witness to Todd about her life as a Christian. He acted like he was impressed and told her a story about his unpleasant young church experience (which he really did not have). But he agreed to attend a service with her. She felt she was winning him to Christ because he was attending and acted as though he enjoyed it. He spoke to the Pastor and told Rev. Mc Evers how much he enjoyed his sermons. He told Sarah he had to drop his classes because of a change in his work schedule. In all actuality his only schedule change was his frequent visits nightly with go-go girls at strip clubs and bars.

Sarah thought he was a really nice guy. He had never tried to take advantage of her. He was very polite. He took her out to eat often. He attended church services sometimes during the week, and on Sundays when he wasn't too tired from his Saturday nightlife. Sarah was giving Todd time to change and believing that the Lord would change his heart. While they were seeing each other, Sarah was more and more drawn to Todd. He was a nice-looking smooth talker. She began to let her guard down and respond to Todd. She was doing favors for him when it was time for church. He would tell her that he did not mean to impose, but his car had broken down. At times, there was some other excuse to hinder her from going to church.

This would happen periodically. It was so subtle that Sarah didn't even notice that this was happening more and more. She was so busy focusing on his problems that she felt that she was just doing what any good Christian would do to help win a soul and show the love of Christ. She didn't realize that absence makes the spirit grow weaker and her spirit was growing weak. Todd was really like the vampire introduced in this chapter. He really wanted someone to become like him, help support his wants and be there for him. He would fix it so there would be no place else for them to go to but him! Todd had a secret. He was **HIV** positive. He had gotten infected by one of the strip club dancers who had a heroin habit and didn't tell Todd. She was young and beautiful. She hid the tracks on her body and she hid them well. She injected herself in some of the most unheard-of places. So since then, Todd felt he had to find someone to pay for what had been done to him.

Now, he liked Sarah, and he felt safe with her. He was sure that she was vulnerable enough by now for him to make a move. So, one night he called Sarah and told her that he had been locked out of his apartment. He said that the super who managed the building was not at home. It was late, about 1:30. He said he had worked late and went with a few of his friends to get a bite to eat and talk. He explained that the time went on later than he had planned.

He asked Sarah if he could come sleep on her couch and he would be up early to get a key from the super if it wouldn't be too much trouble. Well, she was glad to accommodate him, for he had won her trust.

Todd knew his victims well. He always studied them, and he knew that Sarah was always running to the rescue of anyone in need and felt good about it. She had missed services to help him, and he repaid her with overwhelming attention and little gifts, (which by the way were not as big as the gifts she gave him). No one had paid this kind of attention to her in a long time. She had lost concern as to whether or not he was close to making a decision about a relationship with Christ. She believed in his own time he would. She planned to be there when he did and be the one he would love forever.

Well, that night when he came over, he began to talk to her about his past. He said he felt that God and church members could never forgive him if they knew he was causing her to miss church. They would not associate with him because they already looked upon him as a partner of the devil. She explained that was not so. They were just concerned that she remains in the faith and in a close relationship with Christ.

He cried (barely) about the relationship he never had with his father. That did it with her. She was so empathetic that she began to hold him like a mother holds her baby boy. He began to hold and cling to her like a boy would cling to his mother. But she was not his mother, and he was not her son. The passion between them escalated into heavy kissing and hugging and before you know it, they were undressed and waking up the next morning on her couch embarrassed but slightly happy like after the first time. This was before her eyes were opened. It was her eyes that were closed and not his. He knew exactly what he was doing.

A week passed and she did not see him, but he did call her to keep her encouraged. He went to church with her on Sunday and took her to dinner after church. She was feeling guilty about what had happened and condemnation began. One Sunday message was, *"Our Body Is God's Temple."* She explained that this could not happen again and that regardless, they could not be put into the same tempting situations. He agreed, but did try again when they were together. But his future attempts failed.

One day, Sarah was talking to one of her colleagues at the college and brought up his name. Her friend Candice said, "Todd Richards is bad news, haven't you heard?" Sarah surprisingly said, "heard what!"

Todd is a man about town with all the strip club girls and he dated a girl she knew Carolyn and poor Carolyn has been sick since the breakup. Sarah said, "She hasn't gotten over him in two years." Candice said that would be pretty hard since she contracted AIDS from him. Shocked and ashamed, Sarah asked Candice, "How could that be? He is clean and so nice."

Candice said, in case you don't know, everyone who has AIDS does not look like they came from the Bowery! People with HIV can look like anyone of us. That's why it's good to know who you are with."

Sarah thought to herself, "My God, what have I allowed to happen?" She excused herself. She said she was late for an appointment and rushed to talk to Todd. When she was finally able to catch up to him, she asked him where he had been for the last three weeks. He told her he had not been feeling well, not like himself at all. She asked him if he had been to the doctor and he told her he had. She wanted to know what the doctor told him. He changed my prescriptions Todd answered.

Sarah asked Todd if there was something he wanted to tell her but would be too ashamed to say. He was silent for a moment and realized she had found something out. He tried to think fast. He asked if he could come over and talk to her in person. She said she didn't think that would be a good idea. He promised to be a perfect gentleman, but she answered that it was too late for that now! He asked her if there was something she wanted to discuss. She very nervously said, "Todd, I hope what I heard about you is not true for my sake."

He asked as if he didn't know: What have you heard, Sarah? She said, "I think you have an idea. But a friend of mine mentioned you and some of your habits."

Sarah had never heard these stories before because she was not a part of the social set that went to bars and house parties with frat brothers and sorority sisters. As a Christian, she was living the best life she could to glorify God. She didn't know that nice girls could get weak and commit sins and yet love the Lord. She didn't consider that the Lord would still love them even if they had sinned.

Todd finally confessed that he had the virus. He explained that he had contracted it from the girl he thought would add to his prestige on campus and his circle of friends as his date. He tried to convince Sarah that they could handle the problem together. She was hurt, distraught and feeling lonelier than ever before. With a death sentence over her head, she went to her Pastor for consolation.

Ashamed that she could have been so stupid as she said to have let this happen, she explained her plight. Rev. Smith explained that while what had happened was not the right thing to do, that she was not stupid just weak. That had caused her disobedience. He assured her that if she had already repented, God had most definitely forgiven her. And now, she must forgive herself. He and his wife promised to walk with her in what may lie ahead. She would have to tell her parents and her family members, the thought of which terrified her.

Rev. Smith explained that we all fall short of God's desires for us at different times, but we do have an advocate. Sarah felt that if only I had waited, if only I had turned to the Lord in my hour of temptation and asked for help. He would have made a way of escape for me! Rev. Smith said, "We will pray that the Lord has already made a way of escape. Sarah asked, "How could God let me escape after what I have done?"

Rev. Smith answered, "Because He is God and He can do whatever He wants. God doesn't have to condone your sins in order to let you bypass some of the consequences. There are times when we harden our hearts and won't hear when he keeps calling us. Then that may be the only way we can come to repentance. Delaying the pain of our consequences can often delay our repentance and only God knows what will bring us to repentance in order to save our souls. But let us seek God and pray for His will to be done and make known our will for you to be well and whole."

Well, a year went by and there was no trace of the virus. Two years went by no trace of the virus. Every year thereafter, they believed God for her deliverance from the trick of the enemy's plot to destroy her. Needless to say, Sarah learned a valuable lesson. She realized how many young women like herself were not as fortunate as her. As a result of her experience, she started a young single women's ministry in her church to set up safeguards and support for other single women in the church not just for the young, but the middle-aged and older women as well.

Sarah realized how close she came to allowing the devil to destroy her through someone who didn't love her enough to tell her the truth before the fact. **Our** heavenly Father loves us enough to tell us the truth and we ought to obey **Him. In** the hour of temptation, turn to the Lord and He will give you the strength to resist. In fact, He will give you the direction to not allow yourself to get into a place for strong temptation. If you seek Him for wisdom and counsel during and before, He will direct you. Then, your will is to blend into His will. You can make the better choice!

Bitten By Love?

The morning after...

A note lay on the pillow

Revealing itself in the morning light....

Wonder what it says?

Let me surmise

Need to see you tonight you were the answer to my dreams

All I looked for in a lifetime, I found in you...in one night.

Or maybe it says...

I am in love with you, Let's get married

Under the pale moon light Then we will be together

Forever, as a result of just one night…

Okay, the suspense is killing me Why not just open the letter?

I am sure what he has written in the note

Compared to what I have imagined is far better

And the note reads:

I am sorry I was not able to stay

Until the morning light or the revelation of the day Had a great time with you last night

But then who could resist such a beautiful sight...

(Oh, I think to myself as I read the note... He's smitten)

I turned the note over...

He concludes...

Oh by the way; make no plans for our future...

You've just been **Bitten...**

Take Care

By Sonya L. Caldwell

Journal Page

(What Thoughts Did The Holy Spirit Give You In This Chapter?)

"For I am the Lord, Your God, who takes hold of your right hand and says to you, Do not fear; I will help you."
(Isaiah 41:13)

CHAPTER SEVEN

Your Decisions

Your Decisions

Proverbs 16:25 (NASB)-" There is a way that seemeth right unto a man, but the end thereof are the ways of death."

Proverbs 3:6 (NASB) "In all your ways acknowledge Him, and He will make your paths straight."

We are all tempted in different areas of our lives, according to what Satan perceives as our weaknesses. The most critical times for him involve himself with us is when we are about to make a decision. When you have the Word of God to follow as your guide, then your decision should be plain and clear-cut. But when you are in the midst of temptation, the enemy of your soul will always lead you to compromise which brings destruction and confusion. But when you take a stand to obey and follow God's Word, blessings and not curses are yours.

It is time to make a decision to be a Queen or you will resort to being a Concubine, taking second place. If you don't make a decision in favor of what God says, you may end up like Cain, Abel's brother. God had given him a choice after telling him the right thing to do.

Genesis 4:7 (NASB) "If you do well, will not your countenance be lifted up? And if you do not do well, sin is crouching at the door; and its desire is for you, but you must master it."

According to the **NASB** footnote on this scripture, the Hebrew word for crouching is the same as an ancient Babylonian word that refers to an evil demon crouching at the door of a building, to threaten the people inside. Sin is pictured as a demon, waiting to pounce on Cain-it desired to have him. In the same way, Satan through his demonic forces desires to have us. The Bible says he goes forth as a roaring lion seeking whom he may devour *(1Peter 5:8)*. So take time to make the right decision according to God's Word. Why? Spiritual wickedness around us is ready to pounce on us, causing us to make the wrong choices. We are not fighting against flesh and blood, but against principalities and powers against the rulers of darkness of this world and against spiritual wickedness in high places (Ephesians 6:12).

There are many reasons throughout this book explaining why you should not be a Concubine. You only need one reason, and that is the Lord Jesus Christ. You bless or curse yourself by your own decisions. Christ came that you might have life and have it more abundantly *(St. John 10:10)*. Do it the Lord's way and see what the Lord will do. Wait on the Lord and be of good courage, rather than settle for the enemy's short-term temporal gratification; leading to pain and destruction.

Queens throughout history have had to make difficult and unpleasant decisions. Often, it meant personal sacrifices that would be for the betterment of their kingdom, country and loyal subjects. They could not be selfish and think of their own gratification. You, as a Queen, must think of what's best for the kingdom and the subjects under you.

The kingdom may be your household and your subjects may be your children.

It would not be good to bring a man into your domain, who cannot be a true father to your children (if there are any) with a willing attitude. Neither would it be in your best interest to settle for a man who does not want to commit to being a husband-only to satisfy your loneliness. In the end, you will still be lonely for he will not commit to one woman. The true and necessary decision is difficult for the Concubine, but the Queen realizes there is only one decision to make, the one that duty and the law requires. Do it by the book that is the Holy Bible!

You are not your own. You have been bought with a price and that price was the precious blood of Jesus Christ. Don't you think the price paid for you was too high to just be a Concubine? The value of an object is usually denoted by the cost of it. Look at what was paid for you to be born again into the royal family of Jesus Christ. You are a QUEEN, the bride of the king of kings and Lord of lords!!!

God helps your decision-making and even inspires and motivates you through life's events. But only you can make the choice and have the final say. You are worth it! Despite what the devil is telling you, don't let him cheat you out of the life you have been cleansed for and the cleansing that continues. When you come to your journal page, conclude your comments by the signature of your name, Her Royal Highness Queen_____ (your name).

It's Time To Change Masters

"Know ye not, that to whom ye yield yourselves servants to obey, his servant ye are to whom ye obey; whether of sin unto death, or of obedience unto righteousness?" (Romans 6:16/Dickson NASR)

"It is time to recognize who is controlling our actions, which we are listening to; our flesh, the devil, or the word." (Romans 6:1921/Dickson NASR)

"That ye put off concerning the (your)f01mer conversation (manner of life) the old man, which is (waxeth) corrupt according (after) to the deceitful lusts (lusts of deceit); And be renewed in the spirit of your mind; And that ye put on the new man, which after God is created in righteousness and true holiness (holiness of truth)." (Ephesians 4:22-24/Dickson NASR)

"Therefore, if any man be in Christ, he is a new creature: old things are passed away; behold, all things are become new." (2 Corinthians 5:17/Dickson NASR)

It is a matter of fact that those who are in Christ are new creatures with a totally new perspective. The old human perspective has passed away; behold, the new divine perspective has come and is continuing to come. The Greek word "gogonen" perfect tense verb, "has come" with a continuing action. The new creation with the new, divine perspective is a continual, growing; ever expanding experience. It is the experience of being changed into the likeness of Christ from one degree of glory to another *(2 Corinthians 3:18)* by beholding the glory of the Lord. Be ye transformed by the renewing of your mind. Not conformed to this world but trans• formed a new perspective.

Paul tells us again and again that we become the servant to whomever we obey. When we were sinners, we obeyed sin, but now grace has set us free from the law of sin and death. Free not to go on sinning, but to choose the other path of righteousness. Do not give yourself to unrighteousness, but instead give yourself completely to God since you have been given a new life. Sin is no longer your master; instead, you are free by God's grace.

It is impossible to be neutral. Every person has a master. Either God or Satan (sin). A Christian is not someone who cannot sin but someone who is no longer a slave to sin. He or she belongs to God. You are free to choose between two masters, sin (Satan) or righteousness and holiness (Jesus Christ). The Bible tells us that the wages of sin is death (spiritual and sometimes physical); but the gift of God is eternal life.

By choosing Christ as your master, you receive His gift of eternal life new life with God that begins here on earth and continues forever with God.

Make your choice, you really only have one!

Where Is Your Faith?

> *"But without faith it is impossible to please him: for he that cometh to God must believe that he is, and that he is a rewarder of them that diligently seek Him." (Hebrew 11:6/Dickson NASB)*

> *"Now faith is the substance (assurance) of things hoped for, the evidence (a conviction) of things not seen." (Hebrews 11: 1/Dickson NASB)*

We all operate by what we believe, whether it is in fear or in faith. You would respond to God according to what you believe about Him and His word. When God delivered the children of Israel out of bondage and through the Red Sea, Moses went up to Mt. Sinai to receive the Ten Commandments. He stayed longer than they believed he would have if everything were going well. Because they didn't believe he was coming back, they asked Aaron to make them a god of gold to worship. They would never have done that if they knew that their Jehovah Jirah, Elohim God would not leave them stranded like that. They got too impatient and anxious.

So, it is with many of those who don't believe God is going to answer their prayer in the time they think He should. They seem to want God to do all the pleasing. He is not here just to please you or do what only makes you feel good. It really is a trust issue. If the children of Israel had trusted God, he could have blessed them within 11 days, but it took 40 years in the wilderness to raise up a generation of people who would trust God to do just what He said He would do.

If you would trust God for the right mate without compromising your stand **in** Christ, holding your vessel unto honor and not dishonor by sexual impurity, your reward would be greater than your sacrifice. Regardless of how long it may seem to take, when He does bless you, you will say it was worth the wait. So trust in the Lord with all thine heart and lean not unto thine own understanding, but in all they ways acknowledge Him and He shall strengthen thine heart (Proverbs 3:5).

If we can lay hands on our sick bodies and those of others, if we can believe God for the salvation of our children and family members, we can apply that same faith in God to give us a saved mate in the church or save a man out of the world and deliver him to us U.P.S. (United Partner Saved)! You can make it hard because you refuse to say no and not compromise. You must keep your vessel sanctified.

A man will only believe in the God you serve by the stand you are willing to take for Him, by the sacrifices you are willing to make for Him. Anyone you put before your God, kiss them goodbye or look for a spiritual fall. God admits that He is a jealous God and He'll have no other gods before Him. He alone reserves the right to be jealous for he owns you, He alone died for you. How dare you worship another?

To think that your life totally rests in the companionship of a man is to make that desire an idol in your heart. This would say to Jesus that he is not enough. No man wants to hear he's not enough for his woman. A man alone cannot give you peace and true joy in the likes of mere flesh. This would be to worship the creature more than the creator.

Exercise your faith to believe that if ye seek first the Kingdom of God, and its' righteousness all the other needs of your life will be added unto you. This includes a lifetime covenant partner!

It's Your Decision: Queen or Concubine

Queen A female member of the royal house, either the wife of King, or woman who reigns by her own power.

The term "Queen" may also refer to an actual ruler of state such as the Queen of Sheba *(1 King 10:00)* or Candace the Queen of Ethiopia *(Acts 8:27)*. Bathsheba and Jezebel are not called queens, but certainly they ruled with their husbands *(1 Kings 1:21)*. On the other hand, a Queen might be simply the king's favorite mate or wife. From the definition of a "QUEEN," you see she is a ruler and one who holds first place in a man's life. In the kingdom of God, by your relationship to Christ, from a royal priesthood a chosen generation makes you royalty, you are a Queen. First of all, your Father is the King of Kings and Lord of Lords! As his daughters, you are royal, and royalty is expected and commanded not to act as commoners. The man you will decide to be with must understand this and view himself as the Son of the King and not able to act as the common man.

If she is not a queen helping a king, she can be a queen ruling by herself over all that pertains to her. I think Lydia is a fine example of a Queen who was single, yet she ruled as a Queen over her own matters and tended to the work of Christ and the up building of His kingdom.

Lydia was the CEO of her own business in a field dominated by men, yet she was extremely successful. She had her own home with servants and household help who respected her. She had a deep love for God as a Jewish proselyte. She was known to be a devout woman given to hospitality. She opened her home to the saints and was fervent in spirit.

Lydia may have been lonely, just as any other single woman but I believe she was building up her relationship with the Lord Jesus and the saints that she was able to occupy her thoughts with more important matters for her eternal future. She may have had her heart broken, she may have even been widowed, but there is no indication of her ever being married. So most single women could identify with Lydia. Just because she was financially independent and could satisfy most of her material needs, she yet longed for more and found it in Jesus Christ!!

The same can happen for any woman willing to make the work of Christ her lifelong goal, whether she is married or single. The woman at the well had a man and wasn't satisfied, but when she came in contact with Jesus and realized whom he was, she left her water pot and the man to follow him and evangelize the city where she lived.

The devil challenges you to leave your desires to follow Christ and find real life with meaning. Sometimes your calling may be on your job, just being an honest Christian with integrity or organizing helps to build up your community within the areas of your church, for the block or district should be better because the church is in the midst and God's people are conducting the affairs of God to show forth the power of God through "salvation".

The harvest truly is plenteous, and the laborers are few, so look to see where God wants you to plant seeds and then harvest. You have much to offer while you are single, don't fail to exercise the gifts God has put in you for His glory! Work while it is day for the night cometh when no man can work.

My Decision

I am going the straight and narrow

Got my direction lined up

On target like a shot arrow

No more late night calls

No more creeping out late

Only to be shamed by the acts committed

After looking into the face lying next to me

Unknown and not my soul mate

Okay, so things so far have not been so rough A few bumps and bruises here and there

Thank God ... no major head concussion or life threatening contusion (If you know what I mean)

I guess I was able to get out quick

But all along in my ignorance

I never heard the clock in the background TICK...

In the dark, it was cool to play the game

But alas the light from the sun... always revealed my now uncovered shame

Hey, but I had to show that I was not affected

And by the time the night fell...

I was off again heading into the tempters lair

Forgetting about the shame the day before that I had borne

People around me

In the name of adulterous and fornicating love

Getting sick?

You see I know me; I mean knew me...

Well, the old me, you see

And she, well she did what she wanted

And for me to leave that life of crime and sin

Without a trace

Well, I can sum that up in one-word GRACE ...

Ticklers and toys Pleasure by the pound Had it on demand... but not with my mate, well not with my man...

But I know living like that did not take heart

Yet this new way of life... well it took a lot of prayer

A lot of speaking to God Not to mention a bold start

But today I have a choice...

Be someone's toy and enter repeatedly into

Hell's gate or Love me more and just wait...

4 Heaven Sake.

By Sonya L. Caldwell

Let's pray

Dear Heavenly Father,

Thank you for the privilege to cry Abba Father to you. Even knowing that as your daughter I have not always followed your protective and loving directions through your Word. But because you still call me to come boldly to your throne of grace, I ask you now Father to create in me a renewed and right spirit to obey and trust you.

Also help me to realize the strength you have given me to wait for my change whenever and however it must come. I ask not only for my sake but the sake of others who are watching my life that I may bring glory and honor to your name. I desire to walk in the spirit and not in the ways of my flesh, using the weapons you have provided me to bring down the strongholds in my life. I desire to be a vessel in your kingdom unto honor. Reveal to me the treasure you have placed in this earthen vessel that I may unleash it to be used to exalt your name.

Love,

Your Daughter

Journal Page

(What Thoughts Did The Holy Spirit Give You In This Chapter?)

"Trust in the Lord and do good, dwell in the land and enjoy safe pasture. Delight yourself in the Lord and he will give you the desires of your heart." (Psalm 37:3-4)

If you would like to contact Beverly Allen,
please write to her at the following e-mail address:

bevallen777.ba@gmail.com

website:

BeverlyDAllenMinistries.com

RECOMMENDED READING

Kissed The Girls and Made Them Cry

- Lisa Bevere, Thomas Nelson Publishers Sacred Sex, Tim Alan Gardner, WaterBrook Press

Why True Love Waits

- Josh McDowell, Tyndale House Publishers, Inc.

The Pursuit of Holiness

- Jerry Bridges, NavPress, The Navigators

Good Women in Bad Situations and The Grace That Awaits Them

- Beverly D. Allen, Xulon Press

Covenant Dating, The Biblical Path to Marriage

- Beverly D Allen, WestBow Press

Covenant Dating, The Companion Study Guide For Covenant Dating The Biblical Path to Marriage

- Beverly D Allen, WestBow Press

www.ingramcontent.com/pod-product-compliance
Lightning Source LLC
LaVergne TN
LVHW020424070526
838199LV00003B/270